DEALING
WITH HORSES

DEALING

WITH HORSES

J. F. KELLY
A horse dealer for forty years

ILLUSTRATED BY
JOHN T. KENNEY

ARCO HORSE BOOK LIBRARY

ARCO PUBLISHING COMPANY, INC.
New York

Published in the United States by
ARCO PUBLISHING COMPANY, INC.
219 Park Avenue South, New York, N.Y. 10003

© J. F. Kelly 1961

Fourth printing 1972

Library of Congress Catalog Card Number: 72–84392
ISBN 0–668–00977–2

Printed in Great Britain

Introduction

SINCE THIS book was written, over ten years ago, enormous changes in attitudes and circumstances have taken place and as a result one or two passages may appear to be unrelated to the horse scene of the 1970s. However, I have deliberately avoided making any alteration to the text, confining myself to additional footnotes where these seemed to be necessary. My reasons for taking this course were to preserve intact the author's particular style and because I felt that what she had to say was still important, interesting and very informative and would not be improved by any amendment upon my part.

The author, the late J. F. (Jo) Kelly, was a regular contributor to *Riding* and until her tragic death a valued member of the Advisory Panel maintained by the magazine to assist with its readers' problems.

It is not perhaps generally known that J. F. Kelly was, indeed, a woman, a fact which throughout her writing career she took great pains to conceal. Despite having spent a life-time making, schooling and dealing in horses and doing so with considerable success she was firmly of the opinion that no-one would take any notice of 'an undersized silly old woman'. Small in stature she certainly was but certainly not silly. Thousands of aspiring horsemen and women throughout this country and abroad benefited from her down-to-earth and common-sense advice over a period of many years.

This book is typical of her and reveals the practical approach tempered with a real understanding and love of horses, that characterized her work.

I believe that readers will agree that her text should remain exactly as it was when it was first written.

E. Hartley Edwards,   1972
Editor *Riding*,
189 High Holborn, W.C.1.

Contents

CONTENTS

Illustrations

Preface

UP TO the turn of this century the majority of people came into constant contact with horses and learned a great deal about them, almost without realizing it. It could be said that, outside the big cities and towns, the population was brought up with horses.

Nowadays, although horses play an important part in the lives of many keen horsemen and women, we no longer have the advantage of living in an age of horses. As a result, we have to learn from books, and by tuition, the thousand and one things that we would have absorbed almost subconsciously had we been born fifty years ago.

I have written this book in the hope that some of the information it contains will help to fill this gap.

Wey Lodge   J. F. KELLY
Liphook
Hampshire

I

The Horse Dealer and His Business

For many people the term 'horse dealer' conjures up the image of a shifty individual wearing a 'pork-pie' hat, riding breeches and a loud check coat. Usually he bears a reputation which if justified would have put him behind bars at the outset of his career.

For over forty years I have been buying and selling horses, and in my opinion I have earned a perfectly honest living. As one of them I feel I can write with authority on the men and women who earn their living in a similar way.

First let me make it clear what I mean by a horse dealer. Usually he is a man of reasonably good financial standing, with a nice house and probably fifty or more acres of land.

Never confuse him with the travelling tinker who buys and sells 'remnants' of horseflesh as he moves about the country. Those foolish enough to buy from this type of individual should blame their own credulity if they find they have been 'done', and not damn the reputation of horse dealers in general.

I have probably heard of every malpractice ever attributed to a horse dealer, but in many years' experience I have yet to meet a *reputable* dealer who will deliberately misrepresent his horses or swindle his clients.

Now I will try to describe the business of horse dealing as it is today. Like other tradesmen, the horse dealer is out to please his customers and retain their patronage. For most of his income he depends on his regular clients and their personal recommendation to others. No dealer would remain long in business if he continually 'twisted' his clients; so approach him in a spirit of goodwill and confidence, as you would any other tradesman. There is no mystery about him or his activities, but there are legitimate tricks in his trade as there are in many others.

A successful horse dealer must have a number of qualifications; among them, an 'eye for a horse', sound veterinary knowledge and the ability to form a quick and accurate opinion of both man and horse. The old saying 'one man's meat is another man's poison' can be applied in its truest sense to horses, and well the dealer knows the pitfalls in recommending a horse to a new client. A keen horse, full of courage, might be ideal for one man, and yet prove highly dangerous in the hands of another. But if the dealer makes a mistake and sells a customer an animal which is a bit above his ability, he is at once termed a rogue or a twister. Many people will deliberately mislead a dealer about their riding ability, but I have yet to hear anyone admit that they 'shot a line'.

It is surprising how many people say to a dealer, 'Is this horse sound?' This is always a bad moment; he is not a veterinary surgeon, and therefore cannot give an authoritative answer. The best he can do is to say he believes it to be sound. Whereupon the prospective buyer departs and tells his friends how narrowly he escaped being 'done', as there was something very fishy about the evasive way the dealer answered him.

If you want to know if a horse is sound have him examined by a veterinary surgeon, and never pay a high price for a horse without taking this commonsense precaution. Otherwise ask a dealer if he believes a horse to be sound, and take his word if he says 'Yes.'

A man who deals in high-class animals will seldom send a horse on trial, except to a well-known and trusted client. Horses are perishable goods, and may be lamed or his manners permanently ruined by a week of bad management or mishandling. Any dealer will allow a fair trial on his own premises

—so take full advantage of it, and ask for a second trial another day if you are not fully satisfied.

As a rule, a horse dealer does not keep a horse in his yard for long; his aim is to pass his stock on as quickly as possible or they would soon eat their profit. If this point was more generally realized buyers would not ask questions which could be answered only by someone who had had the horse for some time. If you want such knowledge, ask for the address of the animal's last owner, and no doubt he will provide all the information you require. A dealer will never say he does not know, so do not force him to 'spin a yarn'.

And that brings me to how a dealer obtains his horses. Often he takes them in part exchange—these are known in the trade as 'chop horses'. Sometimes a buyer finds out that a horse has been taken in part exchange; when this happens he invariably jumps to the conclusion that there is some snag attached to it. This may be the case, but many people change their horses regularly, either because they prefer young animals or merely because they like a change. Often a horse comes into a dealer's hands because he is no longer up to his owner's increasing weight. There are no 'ifs or buts' about many 'chop horses' and they can be passed on with complete confidence. But what of the others, which change hands owing to vice or unsoundness. The former are usually sent to a sale yard and sold without a warranty. Naturally they do not make a high price, but as they are not warranted free from vice they cannot be returned.

Unsound horses are a curse to every dealer. If an animal has an unsoundness which will render him permanently unfit for work he will be sold for slaughter. But there are many horses that a vet would not pass sound which are capable of many years' normal work. Naturally it will detract from their value, but they are often a 'good buy' for anyone who cannot afford to pay a high price. The dealer will usually mention the unsoundness, and if the buyer likes the horse he would be well advised to have him examined by a vet and be guided by his opinion.

'Chop horses' are a very small part of a dealer's stock. He buys most of his animals at the big horse sales which are regularly held in different parts of the country. Dealers work together, and in this way they gather a good deal of information about the horses that come 'under the hammer'. Many of them have 'contacts' in Ireland who are always on the look out for the type of horses the English dealers require. When these animals arrive in his yard the dealer knows little or nothing about them, apart from the short description which is sent with each horse.

All high-class dealers employ a nagsman*, whose job is to ride every horse which comes into the yard and report on its manners and performance. He is also responsible for the schooling of young horses, the making of hunters and the schooling and producing of show hacks, hunters and jumpers. The nagsman is the most important member of a dealer's staff, and the success of his business will depend to a great extent on the skill of his nagsman.

It is an accepted fact that anyone who buys and sells expects to make a profit on their transactions, but this idea does not seem to include horse dealers. If after buying a horse the purchaser discovers that the dealer has done well out of the sale, the thought will never cease to rankle in his mind. It seems that no one can understand that a horse dealer often incurs very heavy losses, and if these were not offset by a few good sales he would soon be out of business. Most tradesmen count stock as cash, but this cannot be the case if the stock is horses. There is no certainty for a horse dealer until the cash is in the bank. Horses are accident prone and may become a total loss overnight. Horses, especially young ones, often go wrong and getting them right may entail heavy expense in treatment and keep. So why blame the horse dealer for the price you pay him for a horse? If the animal had not been worth that particular sum to *vou*, surely you would not have bought it?

Most dealers are only too anxious to give their clients a fair crack of the whip. The person most likely to get 'done' is the distrustful 'smart Alec' who shoots the dealer a line. But he is the type who always has to learn the hard way, so why should a horse dealer worry about him more than any other tradesman would?

All kinds of people buy horses from dealers, and in the next two chapters I will describe some of them.

The type of dealer described by the author in this chapter is not now in so much evidence, although he still exists in most parts of the country. Many dealers today are women and not a few of them combine dealing with the running of a riding school; additionally a number of the big riding establishments operate a dealing side to their main business.

* The author makes mention of the 'nagsman' in the text and both the term and the individual may be unfamiliar to young riders of the present day. In the big dealing yards that remain 'nagsmen' are still to be found but in the majority of establishments their place has been taken by the ubiquitous, and frequently very competent, girl groom. In all other respects the contents of this chapter are entirely relevant to the modern horse scene and for that reason no alteration has been made to the author's text. Ed.

B

2

The Experienced Buyer

IT is usually easy to pick out an experienced horseman and buyer by the way he approaches a horse dealer when he is on the look out for a horse likely to suit him.

First he contacts the dealer, either by telephone or letter, making an appointment to visit his yard, and stating the type of animal he requires, and giving some intimation of the figure he is prepared to pay.

He will arrive punctually at the time arranged, and as the dealer already knows the sort of animal he is looking for, no time will be wasted on those which are unsuitable.

A horse dealer's yard is his shop window, so naturally his horses will be shown to their best advantage. Their strong points will be emphasized and their imperfections played down. An experienced buyer does not miss much, but he will keep his observations to himself, and his remarks will never be detrimental to the animal he is looking at. He will take it for granted that the dealer knows the weak points of his horses and does not wish to have them pointed out.

When he has seen all the horses which might be suitable he will probably pick out those that have taken his fancy and ask to see them ridden. It is the nagsman's job to ride the horses and show them to the best advantage. If the buyer is looking for a hunter or show jumper the nagsman will jump it over a suitable course.* Only a foolhardy novice would wish to risk his neck on a strange horse without first seeing it ridden. An experienced buyer will watch the horse's performance carefully, noticing every detail and the nagsman's way of riding it. Then if he thinks one or possibly two of the horses may suit him he will ask to try them himself. But he will not ask to try a horse just for the fun of having a 'jolly' over the dealer's fences.

When he rides a horse he will give it a fair test, asking no more of it than the nagsman did. If none of the horses suit him he will not pull them to pieces, but simply thank the dealer for the trouble he has taken, and say that none of them quite meet his requirements. He may add that he would like to have a look at the next batch when they come in.

However, if he has taken a fancy to one of them, he will then bring up the question of price, and ask to have it examined by a veterinary surgeon. These details are usually settled over a drink in the dealer's office.

If the horse is a hunter the prospective buyer may ask to try it with hounds. This is quite usual and few dealers will object to a trial of this kind. A man of this type can be depended on to give the horse a fair trial and not overdo it. If the horse does not prove satisfactory he will offer to pay for his day's hunting, but if it has pleased him he will have it examined by his veterinary surgeon. On receipt of the Certificate of Soundness a cheque will be sent to the dealer and arrangements made to have the horse delivered.

This is the type of buyer who usually becomes a regular and valued client.

* With the enormous growth in the popularity of riding 'experienced' buyers are now very much in the minority. Nonetheless, the description given by the author is important; indeed it is probably more so today than when it was first written.

This example of the 'perfect customer' is one that we should all do well to emulate. Ed.

3

Novice Buyers

IN THE course of a lifetime the term 'novice' can apply to all of us on many occasions. As a rule we are only too ready to admit our inexperience, but for some reason both men and women appear to regard their lack of horse knowledge with a sense of personal shame. To hide this they sometimes air their views on horses and end by dropping so many bricks that a horse dealer has great difficulty in keeping a straight face.

An inexperienced buyer nearly always appears in the dealer's yard unheralded by a previous letter or telephone call. This can be a mutual waste of time, as the dealer may not have the type of animal required.

The story I am going to tell happened many years ago and is perfectly true. Strange as it may seem, this type of buyer is by no means uncommon.

One afternoon a lady and her two children arrived in the yard. She told me she had just moved into the country, and had managed to rent a small field. On the strength of this she had decided to buy a 'family' horse. Her only knowledge of horses and riding had been gleaned from an old pony she had ridden as a child. Quite undeterred by her lack of experience, she was about to undertake not only the care of a horse but also the riding instruction of her husband and two children.

Her manner conveyed that she regarded all horse dealers as shady customers, but had decided to take a chance with me

1. A good sort, but no oil painting

because I lived close by and my advice might come in handy if it was required.

After a great deal of wandering from the point I at last discovered the type of animal she had in mind. This equine paragon had to be capable of carrying her fourteen-stone husband, be a safe conveyance for both children, carry her hunting and go in harness, so that all the family could enjoy it together at week-ends. It must never pull or 'hot up', be easy to catch and completely foolproof in and out of stable. This 'patent safety' must be sound, a mare and not over six years old. And, she finished up, she could not afford more than £50!

I showed her the only animal I had which might possibly fill all these requirements—a cob, fourteen hands, three inches, ten years old, hogged and docked and a *gelding*. He was no oil painting, but a reliable type and a good sort.

Looking him over without enthusiasm she remarked he was not very 'pretty'. Without warning she clapped him on the rump and ran her hand uncertainly down his hind leg, until her fingers came in contact with the chestnut. Straightening her back, she gave me a belligerent stare. 'This horse has a splint.'

'Where?' I asked dumbfounded.

She prodded the horny oval with her finger. 'If you think you can fool me you're mistaken,' she said, warningly.

Never in my life have I been so taken aback, but I was spared the necessity of answering. Her attention became focused on her children, who were surveying the under-surface of the cob with interest.

'If I buy him you'll have to write out a Certificate of Soundness, and don't forget to mention this splint.'

I nodded dumbly but did not explain I was not qualified to issue such a certificate.

I asked my nagsman to ride the cob for her, whereupon she took offence, and assured me sharply she was quite capable of riding him herself. Knowing that the cob was dead quiet I had him led into the school. She scrambled on board, giving a marvellous demonstration of how not to mount a horse. Clamping her heels into his sides she set off at a pace between a trot and a canter. This uncomfortable gait seemed to afford her complete satisfaction. The old cob followed his nose round and round the school, while his jockey revelled in her ability to 'handle' him, as she later described it.

His fate was sealed, and for many years he acted as guardian and nursemaid to the entire family.

This type of client is a headache to a dealer, because he feels he must do something to safeguard them from their own ignorance and inexperience.

A far more exasperating type is the big-headed young man who will 'tolerate no slugs, and can ride anything'. He is usually obsessed by what he calls 'fire', and of course any nag he be-strides must be able to 'go a bit'.

His scanty experience has usually been gained at some small riding school, too financially insecure to dispense with the

2. Thoroughbred 'weed'

doubtful benefit of his patronage, where for a few shillings he can gallop the flesh off every horse he rides.

He is mostly self-taught, and owing to his youth, strength and natural balance has acquired the knack of keeping the horse between himself and the ground. This type is always a great line-shooter and will try to dazzle a dealer with his great knowledge and experience.

A gentleman of this description strolled into my yard one

day. He carried a thongless hunting whip, and emphasized every remark by slapping it against his ill-fitting riding boots.

'Got a useful skin likely to suit me?' he drawled.

'Yes,' I said with conviction, thinking of an undesirable thoroughbred weed standing in the corner box. This animal was hot-headed, gassy and short of a rib, but just the job for him, I decided.

There and then he carried out what he termed a 'veterinary examination', quite overlooking a pair of curbs you could hang your hat on.

He waved my nagsman aside with a lordly gesture and proceeded to negotiate the schooling fences at an incredible speed, leaving most of them flat. Inspired by this shattering performance, he clinched the deal by knocking £10 off the price I asked. I had relied on his 'great knowledge' to realize the animal's approximate value, and was pleasantly surprised to receive almost double.

I watched them leave the yard, and realized with a twinge of conscience that horse and rider would soon be in competition to see which could kill the other first. I consoled myself with the thought that no matter what horse this man bought it would soon become unmanageable.*

I have written about the horse dealer and his clients in the hope that it will help the inexperienced buyer not only to set about buying a horse in a proper manner but to approach a dealer in a spirit of confidence and goodwill. Whether he likes it or not, the novice horse buyer is more or less at the mercy of the dealer. If only he will ask his help he will nearly always get it in full measure. Most dealers will take endless trouble to fix up a novice with a suitable horse at a price he can afford.

---

* Such buyers have existed since the world began. The only difference is that now there are more of them. Ed.

4

Mr. Cash

Many people read the reports of the bloodstock sales in the sporting press. Some of them probably marvel at the high prices which some horses command, and wonder why others change hands for a few pounds. The buyer is entered as 'Cash' against many of these cheap horses, so I shall refer to him as Mr. Cash.

I have mentioned the risk of buying horses from tinkers and such like, but that is nothing compared with the risk of dealing with Mr. Cash. If more people knew of his existence, and how to recognize him, they would avoid much disappointment and financial loss when buying horses.

Almost every district throughout the country has its Mr. Cash, for it is he who supplies most of the meat which feeds our large population of dogs and cats. The bulk of his income comes from buying horses for slaughter, and if his activities stopped at this he would be supplying a useful demand. Unfortunately, many of the useless animals he buys for slaughter can often be sold privately at a far greater profit than they would make in the meat trade.

There are always optimists who hope to pick up a good genuine horse for a song, and Mr. Cash is always ready to encourage them in their belief, and take advantage of their lack of knowledge.

The hopeful buyer usually starts by having a look round the local cattle market, where an occasional horse comes up for sale. Here he eventually meets Mr. Cash, who is known to most

25

people as a horse dealer. Vague rumours sometimes connect his name with unsavoury deals, and it is said that he never has a straight horse in his yard. But the optimist thinks this must surely be an exaggeration, because it is well known that Mr. Cash always has a lot of horses about and they couldn't *all* be bad or he would never get a living.

This is a very natural line of thought, as Mr. Cash does not advertise his connection with the knacker trade—to most people he is just an ordinary horse dealer.

If there were enough old worn-out horses to supply the demand it would not be necessary for him to attend sales in search of animals which can be bought at killing price.

Bloodstock sales are a good source of supply, and there is the added attraction that some of his purchases will make more alive than dead.

To most people it is distasteful to think of young, well-bred horses being sold for slaughter, but for some of them this is the most merciful fate.

There are not many jobs for the thoroughbred 'misfit'— often too light of bone to carry an adult, and too keen and highly strung for an ordinary child or light-weight novice rider, who can only handle them if they are overworked or underfed. Like all thoroughbreds, these weeds need skilled management which they seldom get as no knowledgeable horse-man would buy them, because he realizes that it costs as much to keep a bad horse as a good one.

To return to Mr. Cash. All manner of horses come his way; some obviously lame, others with recurring unsoundness which may pass off for months only to return. The prospect that these will sell well during a period of soundness is encouraging. If they go lame weeks after Mr. C. has sold them who can attach any blame to him? In fact his reputation will be enhanced if he takes them back and replaces them with other duds—plus a cash adjustment in his favour! Most buyers are thankful to get rid of a lame horse with so little loss, and think the hard things they have heard about Mr. Cash are quite unjustified.

Then there are the vicious horses—incurable jibbers, buckers, kickers, rearers and bolters which are bought by Mr. Cash at cats'-meat price. Many of them are good-looking animals which appear a bargain at the price he asks. With his vast experience of 'dodge' horses he knows almost every trick, and there are few horses he cannot 'fix'. If the 'peg' drops out and a buyer creates hell he is always willing to take the animal back and replace it with another. When that also goes wrong, it becomes obvious he has pulled a fast one, but he is seldom on the wrong side of the law, and as no one likes to admit they have been 'had'—especially over a horse—Mr. C. usually gets away with it.

No matter where you find him Mr. Cash's yard will always have an unkept appearance, with a badly stacked, undrained manure heap in a prominent position. Unless he is expecting you his stables will probably be empty, apart from a few casualties and an odd case or two of Strangles. He will be full of apologies and tell you all his horses are turned out owing to the difficulty of getting labour. In actual fact he seldom employs more than one ancient yard man. A few local teenagers are sure to be in evidence, and they provide valuable free labour in return for the joy of messing about with horses and the hope of an occasional ride.

If you want to look at his horses Mr. Cash will take you to a paddock where the best of the knackers are turned out. They may strike you as being quite a useful bunch, but if you want to try any of them there and then you will be disappointed to learn that Mr. C. is already late for an appointment and simply cannot spare the time. However, he will be delighted to have them brought up for you to try whenever it is convenient for you to call again.

One horse in particular may have caught your eye. If you have not already noticed it, Mr. Cash will point out that he is going a bit sore on the off fore due to a kick, and will hasten to assure you that he will be as sound as a bell by the time you are ready to try him. And sure enough he will be—but the thought of a pain-killing injection will never enter your head.

No reputable dealer would touch Mr. Cash's horses with a barge pole, but unbeknown to him one may pass through his hands now and again. The following story is a case in point.

I received a letter from a hunting man asking me to go and see a horse he had for sale. Apparently the horse was a bit slow for him, but he thought it would suit an elderly man admirably.

I liked the horse and bought it. During the time I had him he appeared to be a good genuine animal, and I passed him on to one of my most valued clients, who had him vetted and passed sound.

Shortly after, while galloping in heavy going, the horse put his stifle out. The patella was so loose it was obvious that it had been down several times before. Treatment proved useless and the horse was destroyed.

I had sold the horse in all good faith, and felt very bad about the whole unfortunate business. It was only by chance that I heard later that the animal had come into the district via Mr. Cash.

On another occasion a lady asked me to take her horse in part exchange. She made no bones about telling me its history. Apparently, she had seen it going into Mr. C's yard with a bunch of others, liked the look of it and wanted to buy it there and then. Mr. Cash allowed her to examine it, and had it run in hand for her. When she suggested trying it under saddle he said it had just come off rail and was thoroughly jaded. This seemed fair enough, so she arranged to try it the next day. On arriving in the yard she found it ready-saddled for her. She said it appeared quiet and rather sluggish, but Mr. Cash assured her that it was still suffering from the effects of the journey, and needed only a few more days' rest to put it right.

The price was reasonable, so she bought it. On arrival in her yard it still seemed sluggish and dopey, but the next day it began to show a bit of life and refused to leave the yard, displaying unmistakable signs of vice.

Mr. Cash was dumbfounded when she telephoned and explained what had happened. He urged her to return the animal right away and take another in its place. But the lady did not want any more of his horses and said so in no uncertain manner. Instead, she asked for her money back, and offered to pay the hire for the horse for the few days she had had it. Mr. Cash wasn't playing ball that way—he was on a good wicket and knew it. The lady had tried the horse, found it perfectly quiet, had asked for no warranty and was given none. So that was that.

Undoubtedly the horse had been given a strong sedative before she tried it, and by the time the effects had worn off it was too late to prove anything.

My nagsman rode the horse and found it was a confirmed jibber and rearer. A permanent cure seemed unlikely so it was sent to the kennels.

Dealers are always on the look out for horses which constantly come up for sale. They know they would not do so unless there was something radically wrong with them, so naturally they avoid them like the plague.

Tommy was one of these; every few weeks he appeared in some sale yard. He was a good-looking pony and very friendly in the stable, but it was known to all the regular dealers that he had a habit of bolting for no apparent reason. The last time he came under the hammer Mr. Cash bought him at knacker price.

Soon he was passed on to a clergyman for his son, and for some time they were delighted with him, as he seemed to be an ideal child's pony. Then one day he bolted in a wood for no apparent reason. The boy was thrown against the trunk of a tree and fractured his skull. Tommy was later put down, and it was found that he had a tumour on the brain, which probably accounted for his habit of bolting.

I heard of another man who bought a horse from Mr. Cash and took the precaution of having it examined by a veterinary surgeon, who passed it sound. Shortly afterwards the horse started throwing his head about at exercise, and ended by throwing himself down in a ditch. The animal seemed half-mad and it was difficult to lead him home. The attack passed, and for some time he appeared perfectly normal, then the symptoms recurred. A vet diagnosed the trouble as megrims—an incurable disease which cannot be detected between attacks.

Vets are a bugbear to Mr. Cash, but they seldom 'spin' his horses, for the very good reason he will never have one examined unless he is certain it will get by. If a client presses for an unwelcome veterinary examination, Mr. Cash knows just how to get out of it without arousing suspicion. He will tell the prospective buyer that another client has first refusal of the animal, and until he knows if he is going to buy him or not, he can do nothing further in the matter. Should the interested party enquire later if the horse has been sold, he will invariably be told that it has.

Once in a while Mr. Cash gets hold of a genuine horse and someone will be lucky enough to pick up a bargain, but your chance of doing this is about the same as winning a football Pool.

Stories of Mr. Cash and his horses would fill a book, and those I have told you are true—so be *warned*.

The law relating to the sale of goods, including horses, was at one time based firmly on the axiom 'caveat emptor'—let the buyer beware—since the introduction of the Trades Description Act 1968, however, the warning 'caveat *vendor*' is equally applicable and Mr. Cash must limit his flights of fancy accordingly or find himself in a deal of trouble.

Those unwise enough to have dealings with Mr. Cash are advised to ask for his assurances in writing or, as the request is unlikely to meet with much success, to take along a reliable witness when contemplating a deal with an individual of this sort. Ed.

5

So you would like to be a Horse Dealer?

O<small>NCE</small> bitten by the horse bug, neither force of circumstances nor lack of cash will keep the victim away from horses for long. Many such people drift into horse dealing without knowing the first thing about it. Usually they buy unsaleable animals which soon deplete their small capital and force them to give up before they have really started.

Advice for would-be horse dealers would fill a book, so in this and the next chapter I will endeavour to cover only the main points.

Horse dealing is not likely to be profitable unless a few basic rules are understood and strictly adhered to. In writing this I have in mind the people who can afford to keep horses only if they can be made to pay their way. It does not require a large capital to start in a small way and build up a business.

Until you have become known and have established a name for straight dealing it is advisable to have an independent job and confine horse dealing to your spare time only.

If you have a vision of a stable full of high-class horses, forget it—until you become known you will sell very few of this kind. You must first realize that no business will succeed unless it supplies a demand. So keep your capital intact until you have learned something about the market.

Start by taking every paper which advertises 'Horses for Sale and Wanted'. Study the *latter* carefully. You will find that the demand for high-priced horses is comparatively small, but there is always a steady market for quiet, well-mannered animals at a moderate price. Most in demand are hack-hunters, cobs, Arabs and Anglo-Arabs, and of course a child's quiet pony will always sell well.

The 'Wanted' columns can teach you a great deal about the demand, but you will be completely in the dark concerning the supply, and there is no surer way to lose money than by jumping into a market already glutted. Here you can practice a little harmless deception. Test the demand by advertising horses for sale. It is not necessary to own even one horse to do this. If you receive any replies you can write to the enquirers saying you are sorry but the horse has been sold. In this way you can get a line on the type of animal which is in most demand. It will cost you the price of advertising and the enquirer will waste a stamp.

To some extent your success as a dealer will depend on your ability to advertise a horse attractively and accurately, and your fictitious advertisement will give you practice. A good advertisement should include all essential information, be short and to the point. The following is an example:

'Smart riding cob. Grey gelding, seven years, fourteen hands, three inches. Comfortable ride, good hunter, temperate, snaffle mouth. Traffic proof. Absolutely quiet in and out of stable. Sound. Price £100.'

This advertisement gives a comprehensive description and encourages anyone who is interested to write for further details. The tag 'Suitable for a nervous rider' will often help to sell a horse or pony, but never add it unless it is correct.

Answer all letters and make a note of the writers' names and addresses—they may come in useful later. If you know of a suitable horse you may be able to engineer a sale and draw a commission.

While you are getting to know the market you should take lessons on how to school a horse. Every good-class dealer either employs a nagsman or schools his own horses. This is essential, because no horse will sell well or readily unless he is well mannered and properly schooled.

A nagsman's job is a highly skilled one, so do not try to save expense by acquiring knowledge from anyone willing to offer it free. Go to a riding academy where only qualified instructors are employed, and take a course in breaking, schooling (including jumping) and elementary dressage. Forget everything you have previously learned about schooling and concentrate on learning *their methods*, and when you have mastered them stick to them.

Once you have decided to become a horse dealer attend as many horse sales as possible, but do not be tempted to buy until you know something about the market and are capable of schooling your own horses.

A tremendous amount of knowledge and experience can be gained by attending horse sales if you keep your eyes and ears open. Watch the good-class dealers, the horses they buy and the prices they pay. In time you will get to know them and the way they work. You will learn of 'rings', and even if you do not agree with them the advisability of 'standing in'.

Study catalogues and Conditions of Sale, and learn to recognize a description which carries a warranty from one which does not. Owners do not *forget* to include such valuable information as 'quiet to ride, traffic proof, free from vice, sound', etc. Look for those points which have been omitted and you will avoid buying many 'dodge' horses.

Learn to recognize horses which constantly come under the hammer. Unless they had a serious fault they would not continually change hands. Above all, study the horses, compare them and pull them to pieces in your mind. Pay special attention to the high-class horses—it is only by studying this sort that you will develop an eye for a horse.

Unless you are naturally astute you are unlikely to make a successful horse dealer. If you have this quality you will know when you are ready to make a start by buying your first horse for resale.

c

I have already mentioned that the most constant demand is for hack-hunters, cobs, Arabs and Anglo-Arabs. The hack-hunter will suit the person whose main enjoyment is hacking, but who also likes an occasional day with hounds. They will look for a horse which is a good ride, well schooled and handy, and able to jump a variety of small hunting fences confidently and freely, and he must be temperate and easy to control. The most popular height is from fourteen hands, two inches, to fifteen hands, two inches, and it should be up to at least twelve stone.

Anyone looking for an animal which can be ridden by several members of the family will usually choose a cob. They are also favoured by elderly people. Select one of good riding type with the true characteristics of a cob. Avoid the 'stuffy' sort with a loaded shoulder, these are more suitable for harness work. The most saleable height is fourteen to fifteen hands, and of course good manners are essential. A cob often has a rather large head and strong neck, and only good schooling will make this kind ride light in hand.

Arabs and Arab crosses are always in good demand, principally by people whose ambition does not extend beyond hacking. These buyers are usually the most gullible and many of them think that if a horse is either an Arab or a Thoroughbred it must be good! Their chief need is for a well-mannered animal but not one which is *too* highly schooled, because they seldom know much about the aids. Fourteen to fifteen hands is the most popular height. These 'Arab fanciers' usually fall for what they term a 'pretty' animal. Do not be tempted to sell them a 'pup' at a nice profit—it will do your reputation no good.

I have not mentioned Thoroughbreds because those with bone and substance likely to make middle-weight hunters will command a high price, and the little Thoroughbred weed is a glut on the market, and dear at any price.

The first horse you buy should be one that can give you experience, and for this I would recommend a four-year-old

3. Cob—an easy type to sell

which has been carefully broken and backed and is ready for schooling on.

The easiest way to find what you want is to advertise; state your requirements clearly and how far you are prepared to travel to see and try a horse. Have a good look round and don't be in a hurry to buy the first animal you see. If the price is too high leave it alone—there are always as good fish in the sea as ever came out of it, and you are not likely to make a profit if you pay too much in the first place. The main points to remember when buying a horse for resale are:

1. Never buy a weed. Horses up to twelve stone and over are the best sellers.
2. Avoid a horse which seems nervous or highly strung, or one with a prominent bump between the eyes. This is known as the 'mad' bump—and not without reason.
3. Do not buy a horse with weak conformation likely to cause unsoundness.
4. Never buy an unsound animal at any price, even if you are certain you can get it sound. Enough trouble crops up with horses without buying it.
5. A horse with vice is always a bad buy. *You* may be able to cure it, but the chances are it will recur again after you have sold it, which will reflect adversely on your good name.
6. As a rule, a horse of an unusual colour is difficult to sell.
7. A black horse is often bad-tempered and unreliable.
8. Choose a horse with an all-round pleasing appearance—one which meets you well and passes you well.

Until you have learned some of the pitfalls connected with buying horses it is far wiser to have them examined by a veterinary surgeon before finally deciding to purchase. Not only is this a safeguard against buying an unsound animal but you will gain a great deal of knowledge by constantly watching a vet examine a horse, and in time you will be able to rely on your own judgement with comparative safety.

Read all you can concerning the horse in health and sickness, but do not make the mistake of fancying yourself as a vet.

When you have bought your first horse do not hurry its schooling or you will end by retarding its progress and may have to start at the beginning again. A dealer's horses should not be over-schooled, and their education should stop at elementry dressage movements, or many people will be too inexperienced to ride them. Nothing confuses a highly trained horse more than an inexperienced rider.

All your horses should be schooled over a variety of jumps up to four feet. This will make them more saleable and you will not be likely to part with a potential show jumper without knowing it.

There is always a demand for show jumpers and for some time it has been on the increase, so be sure you realize the full jumping ability of every horse before you sell it. If a horse can get four foot, six inches easily and consistently he is worth producing in a Novice Jumping Class. Showing is seldom profitable, but success will help you and your horses to become known in the right quarter, and many potential buyers are found in the show yard.

Until you can give your full time to dealing do not saddle yourself with more than three horses at the same time. So far I have not mentioned stabling or pasture. While you are learning the trade you can make do by either renting a field or hiring grazing at so much per head. You will need at least one stable and a dry place to keep tack and fodder.

Strict economy will be necessary if your capital is small, so keep your horses out and school them off grass to start with. Schooling takes a good deal out of a horse so supplementary feeding will be advisable. Horse nuts are an excellent balanced feed, or they can be mixed with crushed oats and chaff. The amount required will depend on the quality of the grazing, the time of year, the type of work and the individual animal itself.

In winter it will be necessary to feed a ration of good hay as well. A dealer's horses should be kept in fairly big condition and carry a good bloom. A little extra flesh will hide many minor faults in conformation, and dealers' horses are not expected to be in hard condition.

Poor-quality fodder is never an economy, so buy the best and do not risk your horses going wrong through eating damaged hay, or corn which is out of condition.

Your horses should never be over-fresh or they will not show to advantage, and will be unsuitable for many people.

Never school in an open field. An enclosed school is essential. A level corner of a field where the boundary fence can act as two sides is suitable, and inexpensive timber to fence the other two sides can often be obtained from a timber yard.

Until you have formed an opinion of how your business is likely to progress it is a mistake to lay out any unnecessary capital. I knew a man who started with a small paddock, a shed, one jump made of old sleepers, and two green horses. One horse won a Novice Jumping Class the first time out, and an Open Class two days later. The other won a Handy Hunter Trial. The one jump made of sleepers was the only thing these horses had been schooled over. This is by no means an isolated case and proves that expensive equipment is not necessary to produce well-schooled horses.

Another essential is good tack; this can often be picked up reasonably at horse sales. Saddlery in good condition, by a well-known maker, is an investment. It will be useful to you in your business, and will usually sell well if you want to make a little on the side. Nothing enhances the appearance of a horse more than good well-kept tack.

Keep careful and detailed account of all expenditure, otherwise you may be misled into thinking you have made a profit when the reverse is the case. It is impossible to build a successful business unless it is run on sound financial lines from the start.

After two years of feeling your way you should know if you

have a reasonable chance of making a living as a horse dealer. If you decide against it, after gaining experience on the lines I have suggested, you will not have incurred any serious financial loss, and no doubt you will have had much pleasure and gained a considerable amount of knowledge.

If, on the other hand, you decide to become a horse dealer, now is the time to get down to it and make a start in earnest. You will not be likely to make a fortune, but your interest in horses will never lack stimulation owing to the great variety of animals which will pass through your hands. The people you meet will be as interesting and varied as the horses, and will tax your judgement every bit as much. You will become boss of a business which entails more worries and troubles than most, but in spite of this you will find it's a *great life*.

The information and advice given in this chapter remains as good as ever. Intending horse dealers, when dealing with ponies, Arab derivatives etc. would, however, do well to remember that an animal entered in a breed society's stud book or register, whether pure-bred or not, will be more valuable than one of unknown parentage—this, of course, is particularly applicable to mares. Ed.

6

Establishing a Business

BEFORE giving up your regular occupation it would be advisable to find a suitable house with land and stabling. The first thing to decide is where to start your business. Here you may give considerable rein to your personal preference, because horse dealing does not tie you to any particular district, but you would be wise to choose a county where hunting and riding are popular. No one wants to travel a long distance to see a horse if it can be avoided, so a locality which is approximately midway between coasts would probably be best, as you could then draw your clients from all sides.

It is almost impossible to find a suitable house with land and stabling, so I suggest you forget about the latter for the time being and concentrate on the house and land. If you circulate your requirements among the big house agents you will probably find what you are looking for. Between twenty-five and fifty acres should be ideal for your purposes, and the more small fields it is made up of the better. You will need them to rest the pasture and separate different bunches of horses. Look after your pasture well—there is no cheaper feed than grass.

The sale of certain types of horses are more or less seasonable. Hunters sell best from September to Christmas, after that it is only a matter of replacing animals which have gone lame, etc. It is the same with show horses, the greatest demand is in the spring and it dwindles as the summer passes.

You can save expense by turning out surplus hunters in

summer and show horses in winter. This will also save labour, and both types of horses will benefit from a run at grass.

Next you will have to get down to an item of primary importance—stabling. This can be a real headache, because a yard suitable for a horse dealer is seldom found with the right house and land. Of course, you can always build stabling, but if, at any time, you want to sell up it will probably be a total loss, and may even detract from the value of the property, because no one wants a large range of stables unless they have a use for them.

Probably the best solution is to buy sectional loose boxes. They have the following advantages:

1. You can restrict your initial outlay by purchasing only the number you require, and then add to them as your business grows.
2. If you want to sell out or move they can be dismantled and erected elsewhere.
3. There is always a market for good second-hand loose boxes.
4. If you deal with a reputable firm they will give you invaluable advice over planning your yard so that it can be enlarged when necessary.

These points are all worth considering. In my experience an ordinary builder has no idea how to plan a stable yard, or design stables. It is only after they are built that unforeseen snags become obvious, causing inconvenience and adding to the cost of labour.

Do not be in a hurry to fill your stables the minute they are built. Buyers do not grow on gooseberry bushes, and horses soon eat what profit they are likely to make. If you have been working with an eye to the future you will probably have one or two show horses ready to produce, and at least one useful hack-hunter. Animals of this type can lay a good foundation for your business by getting your name known in the show world, hunting field, at hunter trials and one-and three-day events, etc.

Always hunt a useful horse, and when you have given a show with him take him home, so that his legs will remain fresh and he will keep his bloom. Take an active interest in the local branch of the Pony Club, and be ready to lend a hand whenever necessary.

Many horses are sold through advertising, but sitting at home waiting for replies will soon land you in the 'red'; however, if you go the right way about it you will be surprised how quickly your clientele builds up. Moderate-priced horses may continue to be your main breadwinners, but bread alone is not enough. To provide the jam you will have to specialize in one or possibly two types of horses. I suggest you first concentrate on supplying novice jumpers. Any horse may have what it takes to make a jumper, and they can often be picked up very reasonably. Success will depend on your ability to recognize, in a green horse, the potentiality of a show jumper, and to be able to school and produce him. We all make mistakes, so if your judgement has been at fault cut your loss as soon as it becomes apparent, because you will never make a jumper out of any horse unless he has the necessary 'pop' in him. If he cannot get four feet six inches consistently he will never make a show jumper. The time to sell is when your horse has won in good novice company. Many horses will never improve beyond this, and it seldom pays to hang on to a horse in the hope that he will turn out to be a world-beater.

Animals likely to win hack or hunter classes often sell well, but the supply is usually greater than the demand, with the result you may have them on your hands longer than is profitable.

Another excellent line is hunters up to fourteen stone and over and a few horses of this type are a sound investment. Heavy men are often past middle age, have an assured position and can afford to pay for what they want. Whereas the young man usually has his way to make, and must cut his coat according to his cloth.

4. Hunter up to fourteen stone

Well-mannered show ponies and those suitable for inexperienced riders are always in demand, but unless you have a light-weight wife or family who are capable of schooling them they are best left alone.

Your yard should always be immaculately kept, and your horses look well-turned-out and cared for. Your stables are your shop window and unless you show your goods well your sales will suffer. First impressions are important and will bias a buyer in favour of your animals or the reverse. No one will expect to find a high-class horse in a dirty, untidy yard.

The cost of clothing will have to be included in your initial outlay. This is a heavy item, but if you keep your eyes open at horse sales you can often pick up good second-hand rugs, blankets, rollers, head collars, etc., at a reasonable price.

See that your horse rugs are always clean, head collars soaped, brasses polished and brow bands whitened. Attention to small details go a long way towards making a good impression Your own turnout is equally important. An untidy rider, wearing badly cut clothes, will not improve the appearance of any horse. Plenty of 'spit and polish' is a great aid to a sale, especially if the prospective buyer is a novice!

If a client makes an appointment before coming to have a look at your horses, have those likely to suit him well turned out—well strapped, manes put up, heels trimmed and hoofs oiled. Do not saddle the horse before he arrives; he will want to see it stripped, and apart from this he may jump to the conclusion that it suffers from a 'cold back'. Always have a horse ridden for your client to see before allowing him to try it himself.

You should keep a small field near the yard specially for schooling. It should have an enclosed school, a variety of schooling fences and a set of show jumps, also a level stretch where a horse can really gallop on. Most of your business will be done in this field, so see that it is well laid out and kept tidy.

For schooling show jumpers you must have a set of standard show jumps. These are expensive, but you may be able to find a good second-hand set; they are often advertised in *Horse and Hound*.

So far I have not mentioned the most costly item of all—labour. Once you have several horses up you cannot do without it, because your own time will be too valuable to spend strapping, feeding mucking out, exercising, etc. To start with you can save the expense of a nagsman by doing your own schooling. In a dealer's yard one groom is expected to do at least four horses, so employ an experienced man who is prepared to do this, and be sure to make this point clear before engaging him.

Choose a man used to exercising with one or two led horses. Find out the correct wage for a groom, and do not pay him less than the minimum rate or you will be in trouble with the law.

Cheap labour is always a false economy. Girl grooms may be quite efficient but they do not lend tone to a dealer's yard, and enthusiastic amateurs are worse than useless and will probably ruin your horses.*

Aim at making every client a permanent customer. It is the people who come back year after year to buy their horses from you who will provide the backbone of your business and a steady income.

If you are 'fly' it is easy to fool some people, and you may pull off a few extremely profitable sales, but you will not be able to depend on a steady income derived from regular and satisfied clients.

Keep out of sharp dealing and concentrate on selling straight, genuine animals at a fair profit. It takes a long time to establish a name for straight dealing, and you have only to sell a few 'dodge' horses to lose it.

A successful dealer will not only try to find horses to suit his clients but will realize the importance of finding clients to suit his horses.

One final tip—never refuse a reasonable profit on a horse or he will probably go wrong and end by making a loss.

* In the 1970s girl grooms are a more familiar sight in schools and yards than men. A good man, indeed, is now a scarce commodity and an expensive one as well.

Most establishments, therefore, rely upon female labour and there is no reason today to think that the employment of a girl will result in any loss of confidence amongst the yard's clientele. Ed.

7

How to Breed a Show Jumper—a Theory

Since the war show jumping has steadily increased in popularity; prize money is higher than ever before, and it is now a highly specialized sport.

Proved jumpers command prices unheard of prior to 1939, but the selection of a young horse likely to make a jumper is still a matter more or less of luck.

It will not be long before horses are bred for show jumping, and those who get in on the ground floor and establish a strain which will consistently produce high-class jumpers will find a market for them not only in this country but in every show-jumping country in the world.

Many years ago I started to breed horses on the lines I shall explain in this chapter. The experiment was extremely promising, but the war came before it had stood the test of time. However, I am convinced that anyone with a knowledge of horses and their breeding, and with suitable land and adequate capital, could produce high-class jumpers by employing my method. For the best and quickest results the young stock should be schooled in the way I shall describe in the next chapter.

Success would ultimately depend on the careful selection of suitable foundation stock. Start with six mares with a good and consistent show-jumping record, and have the following qualifications:

1. Height—fifteen to sixteen hands.
2. Age—not over fifteen years.
3. Free from hereditary unsoundness.
4. Good general conformation.
5. Good temperament.

I would mate these mares with pure-bred hackneys; selecting three stallions and sending two mares to each. It may not be generally known that the hackney is a better and more natural jumper than almost any other breed, with ability to jump height rather than width. As a breed they combine activity, strength and symmetry with sound limbs and good feet. In addition, the hind legs have all the qualities essential for a jumper—strength of quarter, well-developed second thigh and big bold hocks with great flexibility.

When choosing a horse for foundation stock I would look for the following points:

1. Height—fifteen hands or over.
2. Quality, balance and good general conformation.
3. Ample bone below the knee and hock.
4. Sound, well-shaped feet.
5. A deep, well-laid shoulder, capable of fully extending the forearm.
6. A light, free mover, with great spring and elasticity.
7. Courage and boldness combined with a good temperament.

I would expect the stock from this cross to inherit:

(a) Jumping ability far above average.
(b) Flexibility and freedom of movement.
(c) Good temperament.
(d) Conformation and balance above average.
(e) Quality, bone and substance.
(f) Sound legs and feet.
(g) Strength and flexibility of hocks.

Some of the young stock might inherit the hackney's inability to spread over a wide obstacle, but correct early schooling should do much to eradicate this, and it should not be apparent in the second generation. In some cases the exaggerated knee action of the hackney would also be inherited, but this is not detrimental to a jumper, and should breed out in the next generation. The stock as a whole might lack speed, but they will be exceptionally handy and easy to manœuvre.

Careful breeding records must be kept from the start. For example the first year's breeding chart would read:

Foundation mares	1——2		3——4		5——6
	:		:		:
	:		:		:
Stallions:	X		Y		Z
	——		——		——
	:		:		:
Year 'A':	A : A		A : A		A : A
	:		:		:
Foals:	1x : 2x		3y : 4y		5z : 6z

Each foal is recorded by the combined number of the dam and letter of the sire. The letter 'A' above the combination denoting the foal signifies the year of birth. All foals born the following year would carry the prefix 'B', and the year after 'C' and so on. The sex must also be registered against each foal.

Provided the first crop of foals are a level lot, the mares can be returned to the same stallions to be covered a second time. Only in the event of both foals by the same sire being substandard would a change of mating be necessary, then another suitable hackney should be substituted.

By the time the third mating was due the 'A' crop of foals would be yearlings. By then, with my system of early schooling (explained in the next chapter), they would be showing signs of what jumping potential they had. It might be apparent that one horse was getting better jumpers than the other two. In that case discard the horse which is getting the least promising stock and send his mares to the horse which is getting the best youngsters.

By the fourth mating the 'A' crop would be two-year-olds and the 'Bs' yearlings. The foundation mares should again be covered by the sire or sires which are getting the most promising jumpers, and the same policy should be followed in the fifth year.

If my schooling system (described in the next chapter) has been used the 'As' will be jumping (free in a jumping lane) obstacles three-foot high with a four-foot span during their third year. At this stage it should be possible to form an opinion of their natural ability. If there is a colt of outstanding merit and good conformation, leave him entire as he will be useful to reinforce the strain later. Colts with no special promise should be gelded at the usual age, and any youngster without jumping ability ought to be discarded as soon as it becomes apparent. Cull and sort the fillies in the same way, retaining only the best.

At three years old all these horses should be carefully broken and schooled in elementary dressage, but on no account jump them under saddle until they are four years old.

If any of the three-year-old fillies are worth breeding from they should first be broken and then covered.

Hackneys stamp their stock more than most breeds, and any filly sired by a hackney is likely to resemble him more closely than the dam. To reduce the strength of the hackney blood the fillies from the first cross should be put to a Thoroughbred. Choose a horse which has done well as a sire of steeplechasers, and preferably one with sprinting blood in his pedigree. It is important to select a horse with the best conformation for jumping.

The three-year-old fillies out of each crop, which are worth breeding from, should gradually replace the foundation mares. After their first foals are weaned, they can then be schooled and produced in Novice Jumping Classes. The breeder can either produce them himself or lease them for two or three

D

seasons. Provided they have proved themselves to be good consistent performers, they should return to his stud and be put to a Thoroughbred of the type already described. The ultimate aim is to produce a strain which carries 25 per cent hackney blood, and the remaining 75 per cent made up from the foundation mares and the out-cross of Thoroughbred.

Breed first for jumping ability, and second for uniformity of type, retaining only the best stock for stud. A good stallion from a foundation mare may be used to reinforce the strain, by being put to an unrelated mare which carries an out-cross of Thoroughbred blood. It will be necessary to inbreed to establish a strain, but the same blood should not recur in any pedigree closer than three generations back. Inbreeding is useful to stamp a type, but it must be remembered that bad qualities are usually more readily reproduced than good ones.

At the end of ten or twelve years the breeder should have plenty of good stock of his own breeding to choose from, so an out-cross will no longer be necessary.

Once he has established a strain the breeder must then work out his own breeding policy, always bearing in mind that jumping ability is the primary aim. Never sell good breeding stock unless it can be replaced by better, and do not geld a promising colt before he has had time to prove his merit.

To attain the best results from this system of breeding it is essential to school the young stock in the manner described in the following chapter.

Isolated attempts have been made to 'breed' show jumpers since the time the author began her own experiment. None, or at any rate only one or two, have achieved outstanding success or recognition and it is generally accepted that jumping ability comes 'in all shapes and sizes' although obviously some breeds; for instance, the French Anglo-Arab; have had notable success in the sport.

On the other hand it is doubtful whether the author's theory has been put into practice and followed to a conclusion as she suggests. In the absence of such proof the theory outlined would seem to be one most likely to produce jumpers fairly consistently. Perhaps someone will put it to the test one day.

Readers should note that in the many instances where the author mentions Novice Jumping competitions, the Foxhunter classes which are now held would be more appropriate. Ed.

8

Early Schooling for Show Jumpers

THE education of a horse intended for show jumping should commence when he is a foal, so that jumping becomes natural to him from the start.

I shall assume the breeder has a number of paddocks which will enable him to run youngsters of the same age-group together.

To carry out my method of schooling each paddock must be equipped with a jumping lane, by which the young stock can enter and leave the pasture. All the basic training will be done in these lanes, so it is important that they should be properly constructed on well-drained soil. Each lane should be sixteen-feet wide and bounded by solid fences six feet, six inches high, with a solid gate of the same height at each end. If the sides of the lane are not solid the horse's attention will be distracted by what is going on outside, which will lead to careless jumping. The lanes must be surfaced with at least six inches of peat-moss, to avoid jarring the horse's legs and feet.

Each lane should have four fixed jumps, varying in height and type according to the age of the youngsters being schooled. It is important that the jumps should be fixed and have a solid appearance, so that the young horse will not be encouraged to take a chance with them. Place them close enough together to control the horse's speed, which should never exceed a canter; this will enable him to collect himself and jump off his hocks.

THE FIRST YEAR

When the foal is three or four days old and ready to go out with the mare for a few hours each day, he should be fitted with a head collar and taught to lead behind her.

Remove all the obstacles from the jumping lane, and allow the foal to become thoroughly accustomed to it as he is led to and from the pasture. At a month old the foal should have learned to lead freely in hand beside the mare. Then providing he is a strong, normal youngster his jumping education can commence.

Place four poles (six inches in diameter) on the ground across the full width of the lane, about ten yards apart. Lead the mare and foal over these, first at a walk, then at a trot. When he is used to them and has learned to look out for them, he should no longer be led, but allowed to follow the mare loose. From the start the foal must learn not to race down the lane. To encourage steadiness always keep the gate at the end of the lane shut, and make the foal wait while the person leading the mare closes the entrance gate. If the gate at the far end is always shut the foal will learn to pull up after he has jumped the last obstacle. This point is important because if he is allowed to gallop straight out into the paddock he will soon become hot and impetuous. For the same reason never send more than one mare and foal down the lane at the same time.

Once the foal is accustomed to the poles on the ground he may grow careless and start to rap them. Check this promptly by nailing gorse along the full length of each pole, but do not raise the overall height to more than one foot. The gorse will teach the foal to tuck his legs up and jump cleanly.

Never sicken the youngster of jumping, and do not send him down the lane more than twice a day—when he is turned out in the morning and brought up at night. If this routine is followed jumping will be connected in the foal's mind with something pleasant—going out to grass in the morning and returning to a manger feed at night. Throughout his training jumping should always be associated with some kind of reward.

When the foal is jumping the gorse-covered poles with confidence and freedom the width of the jumps may be increased but the height should remain the same. Do this by laying bundles of faggots end to end in front of the pole, to form a jump one-foot high and two-foot wide. When he is jumping freely and cleanly the width may again be increased by laying another row of faggots along the other side of the pole. The jumps will then be a foot high and have a three-foot spread. Continue to keep the centre pole of each jump well covered with gorse to prevent slovenly jumping. As the width of the obstacles increase the foal will automatically jump higher in order to clear them, but he will not be overfaced. The jumps should not be made any bigger until after the foal is weaned, If the mare is carrying another foal these small jumps will do her no harm during the first few months of pregnancy.

When the foal is weaned he will join others of his own age group, and his schooling should continue as before. Gradually raise the jumps to eighteen inches in height, with a span of three foot. This will be high enough until the youngster is a year old. Never put more than one foal in the lane at the same time or they will start racing and their jumping will deteriorate.

SECOND YEAR

During the second year gradually raise the jumps to two-foot high with a four-foot span. Variety should now be introduced, but the number of jumps should never exceed four. Variety can be provided in many ways, such as the addition of a guard rail, a ditch in front of a low fence, or a little bank with a gorsed pole laid along the top. Keep the jumps small and solid in appearance, but never overface a young horse or he will lose confidence. During the second year jumping will require more muscular effort owing to the increasing body weight of the animal and the size of the jumps, so do not use the lane more than once a day. If, at any time, a young horse shows lack of interest or staleness give him a complete rest from jumping for at least two weeks. The aim must always be to make the horse enjoy jumping, and this will be defeated if it produces strain or boredom.

A horse accustomed to jumping from the time he was a foal will show what aptitude he has for the game by the end of his second year. If he shows no more than average ability it is unlikely he will make a show jumper, and it would be wiser to discard him for this purpose.

THIRD YEAR

At three-year-old a horse will not be far short of his maximum adult weight, but his strength and muscular development will not yet have reached maturity, so cut his schooling over fences to twice a week in order to avoid undue strain on his legs. The jumps can gradually be raised to three feet with a four-foot span, and as much variety as possible should be added to them, but do not make them unduly difficult. Top every jump with a fixed pole well covered with gorse, so that the horse will learn that he cannot hit them with impunity.

Some brilliant jumpers constantly rap their jumps through idleness and carelessness. A horse with this habit may be cured by using the following method—nail an electric fencing wire along the top surface of the pole and turn the current on before sending him down the lane. After a few shocks he will jump with more care. It is cruel and senseless to use this treatment on any horse if he is unable to jump above a certain height owing to lack of natural spring and jumping ability.

When a horse is jumping free in a lane never put him over any obstacle which is more than three-foot high or he may develop a faulty style of jumping which can be corrected only if he is under saddle.

Towards the end of his third year he should be carefully broken and schooled in elementary dressage which will improve his natural balance. On no account jump him under saddle until he is four years old, but keep him in practice by jumping him in the lane once a week.

FOURTH YEAR

When the horse has been well broken and trained in elementary dressage he can then be ridden over fences by someone thoroughly experienced in schooling and making show jumpers. If he is ready for it he may be produced in novice company at the end of the jumping season of his fourth year. Do not over-jump him at this stage; one or two shows will be enough to accustom him to the environment of the show ring.

FIFTH YEAR

At five years old a horse should be ready to start show jumping early in the season, but do not overdo him before he has reached his full strength and development. A big backward horse may not be at his best until he is seven years old.

Breeders often part with their young stock without realizing their potential value as show jumpers. If they used my method of early schooling they would be able to estimate the jumping ability of their young horses before parting with them.

I realize that many knowledgeable readers will be strongly opposed to the idea of schooling foals in the way I have described. If they will consider the violent antics and capers of a foal at play (often on hard ground) I think they will realize that hopping over a few small jumps in a well-tanned jumping lane is unlikely to cause unsoundness. In practice it will be found that foals take readily to jumping and obviously enjoy it.

In my opinion the muscles, tendons and suspensory ligaments of a foal are stronger, in comparison to the weight of its body, than at any time before it reaches maturity. If this were not so a foal would not be able to keep up with its dam almost from birth.

Personally I do not think a horse is a natural jumper, any

more than a man is a natural contortionist. A man intended for this pursuit is trained from a very early age, and apparently without any ill effects. Jumping employs a combination of muscles which are not generally used by a horse. If these muscles are gradually developed while the body is still light they will undergo far less strain than if the animal is first jumped under saddle at three or four years old. By then the horse is almost at his maximum weight, but his muscles are still immature. He will also have the additional strain of lifting the weight of a rider over a fence before he has perfected his own jumping balance.

I am convinced that if horses destined to be put to hurdling at three-year-old were schooled in this way, there would be far less unsoundness among them, and the same thing applies to hunters, point-to-pointers and 'chasers.

At a time when a great many horse-owners are more sentimental than knowledgeable about their animals the idea of encouraging a horse to pick up his foreleg, by using an electric fencing wire, as described in the section headed THIRD YEARS may be repugnant to many.

Personally, I have never had cause to employ this method and I would not recommend its use. It should be remembered, however, that the author made her living over a long period by schooling and selling reliable, well-mannered horses on a commercial basis. From my own knowledge of Jo Kelly she would never have condoned, and far less practised, cruelty in any form.

During the years in which I knew her she did, in fact, spend much of her time campaigning against curelty, abuse and ignorance. Ed.

9

Cause and Prevention of Vice

ALL vices spring from primitive instincts without which the original wild horse would have become extinct. He was the prey of animals of the cat tribe which crouched in the concealment of bushes, rocks, etc., and sprang on him as he passed. These powerful cats would pull a horse down unless he could buck himself free. Mares defended themselves and their foals by rearing and striking at their enemy, and by attacking with teeth and heels. Stallions fought for their mares in the same way.

These primitive instincts are still strong in the horse today. A strange object may conceal an enemy, so he shies away from it, and when he means to get rid of his rider he bucks. Rearing and kicking are still signs of fear or temper, and when frightened his first instinct is to take refuge in flight.

Foals are not born vicious, but they practise all the vices in play. A great deal can be learned about vice by watching the behaviour of young horses at grass.

Most vice can be attributed to either bad training or weak horsemanship, and the cause can usually be found under one of the following headings:

1. Breaking a horse when he is in poor or weak condition.
2. Hurried breaking.
3. Allowing playful vice to go unchecked.
4. Too much corn.
5. Too little exercise.

57

6. Lack of tact.
7. Weak horsemanship.

BREAKING WHEN IN POOR OR WEAK CONDITION

Never start a horse's training when he is in poor or weak condition. In this state he will not have enough strength to put up much resistance, and because he gives no trouble he will be hurried on from one lesson to another before he has had time to fully absorb any of them. Because he seems so quiet he will be backed before he is ready for it, and so long as he remains in a weak condition he will give little or no trouble. However, when he grows stronger it will not be long before he pits his strength against his rider.

Always spend sufficient time on each lesson to ensure that it is carried out from habit formed by constant repetition, otherwise the horse may suddenly resist control, and then the rider will find himself on a virtually unbroken animal.

Even if the jockey is not unseated the horse will have learned that he can buck, kick or rear when he is under saddle. He is not likely to forget this in a hurry, and will probably give a repeat performance another time. The only way to undo damage of this kind is to remake the horse from the beginning.

HURRIED BREAKING

The necessity for constant repetition of every lesson cannot be over-stressed. A horse is a creature of habit and has an incredibly long memory, so each lesson must be repeated correctly until it is carried out automatically and becomes permanently fixed in the horse's mind. Vice may also start through boredom which can be avoided by frequent changes of direction on the lunge or long reins, interspersed with short periods of rest. It will also help to keep the horse interested if he is worked over cavalettis[1] or one or two poles laid on the ground.

[1] Stout poles raised from the ground to an overall height of twelve inches.

Never try to train a horse in an open field, always use an enclosed school—he will not be so difficult to control, and if he breaks away he can be caught before he realizes he is loose. It is also easier to keep his attention in a school as there are no outside distractions.

Once a bit is in his mouth a horse must learn from the start that he is 'on duty' and no capers will be tolerated. If he plays up check him promptly and sharply with rein and voice, always using the same tone for a reprimand. A show of vice must never be allowed to go unchecked because the horse must be made to realize that he is under control. Unless he learns this on the lunge and in long reins it is unlikely that he will submit to discipline when he is ridden.

CHECK PLAYFUL VICE

It is impossible not to be amused by the antics of a fresh young horse on the lunge. Unfortunately what starts in play will often be repeated in temper, and the trainer who allows a horse to play the fool may suddenly find himself involved in a trial of strength, but once the horse realizes the trainer is in complete control his confidence will increase. Without confidence and respect for the man who is handling him, a horse is ill at ease and may show resentment through nervousness which ends in a display of vice. A horse's confidence can be gained by treatment which is always consistent.

Do not bribe a young horse with tit-bits; it will achieve nothing useful, and is likely to make him saucy and in the end spiteful. If he has worked well reward him with a short rest, a pat on the neck and a cheerful tone of voice. The voice is a valuable asset in handling horses and they are extremely sensitive to tone, so do not habitually speak to your horse as if he were a criminal, or he may soon become one. Always use the same tone of voice in connection with punishment, and soon the voice alone will suffice. Give short, sharp commands,— 'Walk', 'Trot', 'Canter', 'Whoa' and 'Back'. If they are always repeated in the same tone it is surprising how soon a horse will come to understand them. Never give a command unless you intend it to be carried out, otherwise the horse will become confused and will not connect the word of command with the action it demands.

TOO MUCH CORN

Too much oats will effect a young horse in the same way that too much alcohol effects a man—he will become irritable, belligerent and thoroughly irresponsible. During his training and schooling it is wiser to cut out oats entirely, and feed horsenuts in its place. This is a balanced ration without the heating effect of oats. Many vices are caused through an inexperienced feeder giving a horse more oats than he can stand without getting above himself.

TOO LITTLE EXERCISE

It is natural for all young things to be full of life, energy and high spirits, and a horse is no exception. During his breaking it is the usual practice to keep a horse stabled. As a result of this unaccustomed confinement he becomes overfresh and excitable when he is taken out. In my opinion it is far better to turn the horse out to grass for a few hours each day throughout his training and early schooling. This will enable him to work off his natural high spirits and make him more amenable to restraint and discipline. If it is impossible to turn him out divide his work into two periods a day of an hour and a half each. The majority of his work should be carried out at a slow pace, so each lesson can be gradually increased to two hours as he becomes fitter and stronger. The boredom of standing long hours in a stable account for the development of many vices, especially in a young horse which has always been used to liberty.

LACK OF TACT

Tact is essential to the successful handling of horses, especially young ones, and those who employ it will seldom be troubled by a display of vice in the animals they train.

The early lessons should be so simple that the horse cannot fail to understand what is required of him. Many vices start because the horse becomes confused and cannot interpret the trainer's wishes. This will not happen if the horse is thoroughly grounded in lunging and long reining, and has learned to obey simple commands, starting with 'Whoa' and 'Walk on'. Keep him interested in his work by introducing as much variety as possible and do not overtire him.

Until he is accustomed to the breaking tackle do not rein him up too tightly with check-rein, side-rein or martingale. If he is forced to carry his head in an unaccustomed position for a considerable period it will cause pain and stiffness in the muscles of the neck, and sooner or later the horse will rebel. Good head carriage should be acquired gradually so that pain and discomfort is avoided.

Always handle a young horse firmly and quietly. If he is difficult never lose your temper and shout at him or strike him; this will only confuse and frighten him. Persist quietly in whatever you want him to do, and never give in through lack of patience. Be consistent, and if you check him for a fault one day do not let it pass unnoticed the next.

At the end of each training session allow him to crop a few mouthfuls of grass so that he returns to the stable feeling settled down and calm. It is difficult to know what goes on in a horse's mind, but I am convinced that a happy, confident animal is far easier to train than one which has been forced to submit through rough and forceful handling. Rough handling during breaking will bring out the worst in any horse, and never forget that what he does once he will be likely to do again.

A horse learns almost everything by memory and habit, and will learn bad habits more readily than good ones. Never follow exactly the same routine each day—for example—if a horse is always allowed to turn into the yard when he reaches the gate, it will not be long before he refuses to pass it. If possible exercise on a different route every day so that he does not become accustomed to taking certain roads. Repetition of this kind often lays the foundation for jibbing.

Until a horse is well schooled and reliable never mount him as soon as he is led out of the stable. This is the time when he is most likely to buck, so give him a little work on the lunge first. It is easier to prevent vice than to cure it, so anticipate circumstances which may cause trouble before they arise, and avoid them whenever possible. This is the secret of *tact* in handling horses.

WEAK HORSEMANSHIP

A gay high-couraged horse is not a suitable mount for a weak, inexperienced rider, who, from nervous anticipation will check him constantly and unnecessarily until he rebels. When this happens the horse usually discovers that he is 'best man'; an idea which may be extremely difficult to get out of his head.

A novice rider should always choose a well-schooled horse with a placid nature. On this type of animal they can lay the foundation of *horsemanship*, without which it is impossible to either prevent or cure vice.

10

Suggestions for Curing Vice

Vice in a horse is an action prompted by temper and wickedness and should not be confused with the same action prompted by high spirits. The vicious horse intends to rid himself of his rider and will use strength and defiance to achieve this end. To cure him requires an understanding of horses, a strong independent seat, a steady nerve, determination and endless patience. Without these qualities more harm than good will result, and the element of danger will be increased.

The most common vices are bucking, kicking, rearing and jibbing. Habitual shying and bolting are also vices but come in a different category. Many methods have been used to cure vice with varying success, but here it is only necessary to explain those most likely to prove successful when employed by a horseman of average ability. To avoid disappointment it should be realized that if a horse is sent to a professional breaker for corrective training he may return apparently cured, but in many cases the vice will return when he is again ridden by the same person who allowed him to develop it in the first place. But if that person can carry out the corrective training himself, then there is every chance that the cure will be permanent. With this in mind I shall explain only those methods most likely to prove successful when carried out by a reasonably competent rider.

BUCKING AND KICKING

Both these vices can be dealt with in the same way, because it is impossible for a horse to do either effectively unless he can get his head down. To prevent this the following extra equipment will be necessary:

1. A bearing-rein bit. (Correct size for the horse's mouth.)
2. A separate head-piece.
3. Strong overcheck. (Bearing-rein).
4. Two bearing-rein droppers.
5. One strong steel 'D'.

Stitch the bearing-rein droppers on to an ordinary snaffle bridle in the same position as they are used on a driving bridle. Fix the 'D' securely on top of the pommel of a riding saddle. Buckle the bearing-rein bit to the separate head-piece and adjust it on the horse's head so that the bit lies just below the corners of his mouth. Put the snaffle bridle over this and adjust the bit so that it lies below the bearing-rein bit. Attach the overcheck to the near side of the bearing-rein bit, take it up the cheek, through the dropper, along the near side of the neck to the saddle; thread it through the 'D', then take it back on the off side in the same way, finally attaching it to the off side of the bearing-rein bit. Adjust the check-rein so that the horse cannot get his head down low enough to buck or kick. Nothing will be gained by reining him up tighter than this; it will only cause him discomfort and fray his temper. A standing martingale may be used as well if the horse is generally ridden in one.

Take the horse into an enclosed school and work him on the lunge or long reins, but do not mount him until he is thoroughly accustomed to the action of the check-rein. Whenever he lowers his head to buck the check-rein will check him sharply, and in time he will connect bucking with pain and discomfort. The same thing applies to kicking.

Once he is used to the overcheck he may be ridden. The rider must give him a completely free head whenever he bucks

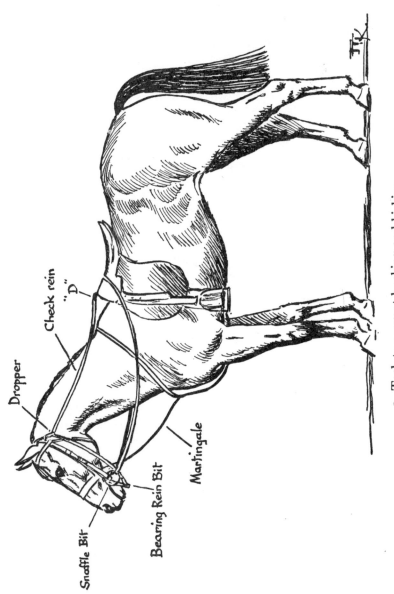

Check rein

Dropper

"D"

Snaffle Bit

Bearing Rein Bit

Martingale

J.K.

5. Tack to prevent bucking and kicking

or kicks, allowing the check-rein to stop him, but the voice should be used in a tone of reprimand to coincide with the action of the bit. The reins of the snaffle bridle will only be necessary to guide the horse and to control his speed.

Work him in the school every day until he has associated bucking and kicking with pain and discomfort. Once he connects cause with effect it will not be long before he gives up the habit. Then he may be ridden outside the school wearing the check-rein.

How long it will take to cure him will depend on his temperament and how firmly the vice is established. At least two months should elapse before the check-rein is discarded, and then only if the horse has shown no sign of the vice for a considerable time. Before finally leaving the check-rein off slacken it a little more each day until the horse is unaware of its presence.

During corrective training feed horse-nuts in place of oats and see that the horse is kept in fit condition. If he is allowed to become poor the vice will probably return when his condition improves.

Warning. Never jump a horse in a check-rein.

REARING

This is a most dangerous vice because there is always a chance that the horse may slip and fall on the rider. It is also the most difficult to cure, as no tack has yet been devised which makes it impossible for a horse to rear. Many methods of curing this vice have been tried but few have met with permanent success. However, the following method has given reasonably good results.

Before commencing corrective training have the hind shoes removed. The horse should then be worked on grass as much as possible, but if he plays up on a slippery surface he will have a better foothold.

Ride the horse in a snaffle bridle with a fairly short standing martingale. If he takes a strong hold use a dropped noseband, but do not put a curb bit on him, because this is often instrumental in causing the vice in the first place.

The rider should wear a pair of hunting spurs and be fully conversant with their correct use. The points on the rowels must be sharp but not long. Avoid blunt spurs or dummy rowels; these bruise the horse's sides and the pain caused does not cease with the punishment. As a safety precaution the horse should wear a strong neck strap or stirrup leather round his neck. The rider should hold this when the horse rears and give him a completely free head. Corrective training should include elementary dressage exercises carried out in an enclosed school.

Be prepared for the horse to rear, and as his forelegs leave the ground apply both spurs sharply and maintain the pressure until he comes down. Few horses will continue to rear under these conditions and will usually bound forward. Punishment must cease promptly as his forefeet touch the ground. Do not apply the spurs at any time except when he rears, and always use a tone of reprimand as he goes up which coincides with the pain caused by the spurs. To be effective the punishment must be prompt and sharp, and it is essential for the rider to have a strong independent seat and good nerve. When the horse connects rearing with pain he will not continue the practice for long.

Electric spurs are well worth trying, and often prove more effective than those in general use. Also they are more humane, because once the shock has passed there is no soreness left in the horse's sides.

If he is going kindly reward him with a friendly word and a slap on the neck. Even a vicious horse will often respond to a kindly word and a cheerful tone of voice. Talk to him and do not reserve your voice for a reprimand only.

When he has shown no tendency to rear for a month or six weeks he may be ridden outside the school, but avoid any place where the surrounding conditions will give the horse an advantage. Do not ride him without spurs, but never use them unless he rears.

This method is not without risk to the rider, but I know of none which is.

JIBBING

Many young horses hesitate or stop because they are uncertain or confused, but this should not be regarded as jibbing, and it can usually be overcome by quiet firm handling. If a little tact is used the incident will not remain in the horse's mind. The vicious jibber defies his rider either by refusing to go in any direction or only in one. If he is forced he may become violent; this is not only disconcerting, but is likely to lead to the development of other vices.

To cure a confirmed jibber requires endless time and patience. Everything possible should be done to confine his defiance to passive resistance. Start by working the horse in a school on the lunge or long reins. If he jibs drive him on quickly in any direction he will go, thus making him think he is obeying the trainer. Before mounting exercise him thoroughly in this way. No special tack is required, but a packet of cigarettes and some sandwiches may add to the comfort of the rider, as he will probably have to spend a considerable time in the saddle.

Do not give the horse anything to eat or drink for an hour or two before he is ridden, then take him to a quiet place away from traffic, etc.

Be prepared for him to jib and at the first sign say 'Whoa' in a tone of command. Give the horse the impression that he has stopped because it is the wish of his rider. Make him stand still and stand properly—head up and equal weight on each leg. Keep him standing like this until he is not only willing but eager to go in any direction. It may take hours of inactivity, just sitting on the horse's back, but during this time he must be made to understand that he is obeying his rider's will.

When it is evident that he is bored, tired and hungry and anxious to go anywhere, ride him away from home. If he puts up no opposition take him back to where he jibbed and ride him backwards and forwards past the place. If he jibs again another session of standing still will be necessary. Repeat the lesson whenever he shows signs of nappiness or is obviously about to jib.

Always give him plenty of work in the school before riding him, because lack of work and over-freshness is often the cause of this trouble. It may take months to cure, but with time and patience jibbing and nappiness are curable.

SHYING

Common causes: defective eyesight, over-freshness, fear, vice.

Habitual shying is counted as a vice because it endangers the rider, but it is very seldom prompted by viciousness. If a horse constantly shies have his eyes examined by a veterinary surgeon who will prescribe treatment if they are defective.

Shying is sometimes a form of playfulness due to over-freshness which may be caused by too much corn or too little work. Check the horse quietly but firmly whenever he shies, but do not punish him. A fresh horse will often shy at traffic and ignore it after a period of exercise. It is a mistake to punish him with whip or spur for this type of shying, because he may learn to connect traffic with pain and become genuinely afraid of it. Many horses are made permanently traffic-shy by this kind of mishandling. Check him firmly with rein and voice, and if possible take the edge off his freshness in a quiet place away from traffic.

Genuine fear is a common cause of shying, and naturally some horses are more nervous than others. Never inflict pain on a frightened animal; it will only increase his terror. He is more likely to be cured by increasing his confidence. First give him a reasonable amount of work in a school or some quiet place, then *lead* him out in a snaffle bridle and allow him to see as many different sights as possible. He will gain confidence more quickly if he is led than he will if he is ridden. Do not force him up to an object he is afraid of; allow him to stand well away and have a good look at it. Make much of him and encourage him with a quiet confident voice. With patient handling he will gain courage and go up to it, then touch it yourself and let him realize that you have no fear of it.

When dealing with an exceptionally highly strung nervous horse lead him about and visit such things as tractors at work, a goods yard, brewery yard, bus depot, saw mill, cattle market, level crossings, railway bridges, etc. Remember nothing will be gained by frightening a horse half out of his wits, only time and patience will improve his confidence and courage. When leading a horse towards an object he is afraid of do not keep looking back at him, this will make him even more nervous. If you walk calmly ahead of him he will probably follow and forget his fears. Lack of understanding and rough handling can ruin a nervous horse for life.

If viciousness is the cause of shying a horse will do it with the intention of getting rid of his rider, and his sudden swerve is usually accompanied by bucking, kicking or rearing. If the trainer thinks fit he can use the corrective methods already described for these vices. But he should be certain that vice is the cause, bearing in mind that this is seldom the case.

BOLTING

The term bolting or running away has almost died out. Today, horses see and hear such a variety of things that they are seldom frightened by anything to the point of bolting. However, should this occur the rider must on no account lose his head. A horse frenzied by fear is not amenable to control, but a firm hand and a quiet voice may reassure him, whereas rough handling will only add to his fear. If time and conditions permit try to pull the horse round so that he gallops in a circle. He will probably not be looking where he is going, so is liable to run into anything in his path. When he stops he may plunge violently, so slip off him quickly and get to his head.

Whatever caused the horse to bolt should be avoided for as long as possible to give him time to forget it. This also applies to the place where he was frightened. If it can be arranged it is far safer to find out his future reactions to the same thing when he is being led.

A horse which makes a habit of running away is a thoroughly unsafe animal, and the chance of curing him is not worth the considerable risk involved.

Many horses take 'a strong hold' and are difficult to control, but they are not running away. The cause may be found in a decayed tooth, a wolf tooth, lampas or some other abnormality in the mouth which should be examined by a veterinary surgeon. If the horse's mouth is healthy, then the trouble is probably caused by the use of an unsuitable bit, and the problem will seldom be solved by substituting one which is more severe. All the different types of snaffles should be tried, not forgetting the rubber snaffle, in which many hard pullers go well. If none of them prove satisfactory try them all again in conjunction with a dropped noseband.

Pulling is often caused by bad head carriage; this can be improved by good hands, schooling and dressage training.

A rider's hands are sometimes as hard as iron, but contrary to the old saying a horse's mouth very seldom is. Also remember that a hard-pulling rider makes a hard-pulling horse.

A vicious horse is usually an unhappy animal, so be patient and try to understand what is going on in his mind. In the vast majority of cases *the trouble with horses is people.*

The reference to a 'bearing rein bit' may puzzle those not familiar with the device. Usually it is a light, fairly sharp snaffle, often made with very small bit rings and is fitted above the mouthpiece of the ordinary snaffle and well up in the mouth. A similar restraint can be achieved, without using an extra bit, by attaching a piece of thin cord to the normal bit rings, passing it upwards through the loops of the browband and then securing to the dees on the front arch of the saddle. Ed.

II

Clipping and Trimming

Nature intended the horse to live out all the year round, so he grows a thick winter coat intermingled with long wiry hairs off which the water runs, and this provides a wonderful protection against cold and wet. However, it is quite unsuitable if the horse is required for fast work, because it will make him sweat excessively and take a considerable time to dry. This will not only render the horse liable to catch cold but will undermine his strength and condition.

The summer coat starts to fall out in August, and by the beginning of October it is fully grown and set. Hunters are usually clipped in October for the first time in the season. A horse should be brought up from grass at least three weeks before he is clipped. This will give him time to become acclimatized to the change in living conditions, and to get the coat reasonably clean by regular strapping.

As this chapter is to help those who have never clipped a horse before, I will assume they will start on a quiet horse that will stand still. An animal which is difficult to clip is not suitable to learn on.

EQUIPMENT REQUIRED

A week before the horse is to be clipped assemble and check the following kit:

A really good stamp of working
pony for which there is always
a ready market.

Eventing is very much the 'in'
sport and horses that show
talent in this field will
command high prices.

Above This is a high-class show cob, but animals of this type make good all-rounders and are the backbone of many small dealing yards.
Below A part-bred Arab that not only looks nice but performs as well. Arabs and their derivatives are always popular amongst the riding public.

Above A group of very typical Pony Club types. Well-mannered ponies for children are always in demand and do not require the feeding and attention which has to be given to horses of Thoroughbred extraction.

Below A top-class young hunter whose conformation is difficult to fault. This is the make and shape that the intending dealer should train himself to recognise.

Above Schooling a likely youngster in the jumping paddock. A horse that jumps competently increases considerably in value.
Below A practical family pony.
This active fellow is a pure-bred New Forest.

1. Clipping machine—electric or hand-driven.
2. Two sets of body blades.
3. Two sets of leg blades. (If legs are to be clipped.)
4. Curved trimming scissors.
5. Small comb for pulling mane and tail.
6. Can of Three-in-One oil for machine and knife.
7. Old dandy brush for cleaning clipper head.

A clipped horse will need:

1. Two rugs—one for day use, one for night.
2. One or two wool blankets, according to the weather.
3. Roller and wither pad. (Breast girth if necessary.)
4. A set of wool stable bandages.
5. Tail bandage.

If the clothing has been stored hang it in the sun to air. Check stitching on all straps and buckles.

Make sure the clipping machine is in good order, well oiled and running freely. It is impossible to clip a horse well unless the knives are in perfect condition, sharp, free from rust and no teeth missing. Always keep a spare set of body and leg blades; they break easily if knocked or dropped. The knives work fast and get very hot, so frequently brush them free from hair and oil. Wipe off surplus oil or it will mark the horse's coat.

ESSENTIAL POINTS

Before starting to clip the following points should be understood:

The clipper head holds the blades, and the two blades together are called the knife. To use the knife correctly the plate at the back must lie flat against the horse's skin. Never press the front edge of the knife down into the skin; this causes pain and will impede the working of the blades. Whenever possible clip in long sweeping lines, each one just overlapping the last. Do not push the knife faster than it will cut. Avoid clipping over loose folds of skin without first stretching them flat with the free hand, and be careful not to prod the horse with the corners of the knife. An assistant to hold a leg up when required will be helpful but not essential.

If the clipping machine is hand-driven the success of the operation will depend to a certain extent on the person turning the handle. He should place the machine behind the operator and slightly to the left or right, according to which hand he is clipping with. If the machine is too close the driving chain will not run freely within the cable and the handle will be difficult to turn. If it is too far away the operator cannot reach his work. The handle must be turned at an even steady pace without any jerking or the knife will cut unevenly.

Speak to the horse while he is being clipped, make much of him from time to time and give him an occasional rest.

Always clip in a good light.

SADDLE PATCH AND STOCKINGS

Never clip the hair under the saddle; it acts as a pressure pad and helps to prevent galls. Neither should the hair on the legs be clipped short, or the horse will be liable to get mud-fever and cracked heels. The long hair left on the legs are called stockings. A cross-bred horse often carries an excessive amount of hair on the legs which detracts from a smart appearance. When the horse is clipped for the first time in the season some of this may be removed by clipping the legs with a leg knife. Do not clip the legs more than once each season. A thorough-bred will only require trimming round the fetlocks and heels with a leg knife or trimming scissors.

HOW TO SHAPE THE SADDLE PATCH AND STOCKINGS

An experienced clipper and trimmer will shape the saddle patch and the top of the stockings as he clips, without first

6. Hunter—correctly clipped and trimmed

marking them out, but to avoid mistakes the novice would be well advised to mark them out before starting to clip. To do this place the saddle which the horse will wear on his back in the correct position. (Without stirrups or girths.) Set the knife in motion and draw it backwards down the horse's shoulder until he is used to the feel of it moving against his skin. Then turn the knife on its side with the back plate against the edge of the saddle and clip round the outline of the saddle, which can then be removed. Make the finished saddle patch one inch smaller all round than the outline. The edge of the long hair should be finished in a clean line. To do this turn the knife again on its side and trim wherever necessary.

STOCKINGS

To mark these use the knife in the same way as for the saddle patch. The stockings on the forelegs should start about three inches below the elbows at the back. Mark a straight sloping line from there to the centre front, where they should be three inches longer than at the back. Mark the insides of the legs to match. Clip a little lower than the marking line, and finish the top of the stocking with a clean line.

The hind stockings should be marked the same way. It will give an illusion of extra breadth and strength to the leg if the hair is cut straight across about three inches below the stifle. If a sloping line is preferred, start about three inches lower at the back. Mark the inside of the legs to match. Finally finish the top of the stocking by clipping a clean line just below the marking line.

HOW TO CLIP THE BODY

Start on the outside of the foreleg above the top of the stocking and work upwards over the shoulder, then up the neck as far as the head. Take great care not to clip the hair of the mane. Next do the front of the neck and breast. To clip between the forelegs and behind the elbow an assistant should pick up the foreleg on the side being clipped and pull it forward as far as possible. This will stretch the loose skin behind the elbow and give a level bearing for the knife.

Next clip under the belly, over the ribs and round the saddle patch. If the horse is ticklish about the belly and flank the assistant should hold up the foreleg on the side being clipped. Support the leg by placing the hand under the front of the hoof, the horse will then be unable to lean his weight on the assistant.

When clipping the flank a hand should be placed behind the loose skin where the hind leg joins the body, in order to give a firm bearing for the knife. It is very easy to cut or pinch the skin here and great care is necessary.

Shape the top of the hind stocking, then clip over the quarter and loin. The coat at the top of the tail should be clipped in a short 'V' with the point upwards and central.

One side of the horse will now be finished and the other side must be done to match.

THE HEAD

Clip the head last. Before commencing, turn the horse round so that a good light falls on his head. Owing to the many planes and angles on the head it is not easy to keep the knife lying level, however, with care it is quite possible. Do not hurry the job, work carefully round the eyes and avoid clipping the eyelashes.

To clip the outside of the ear hold the tip and clip from the base upwards. The hair inside the ear may be trimmed, but should not be clipped close as it provides protection against dust, etc. Finish the ear by holding the two edges together and clipping down the front.

CARE AFTER CLIPPING

There is sure to be a certain amount of grease in the horse's coat after he is clipped. To get rid of it put a blanket on under the saddle and give him a sharp canter to make him sweat. When he returns he should be well strapped and wisped, then if he is well in himself he should carry a good bloom. Remember that no amount of strapping will produce a really good bloom unless a horse is clean inside as well as out.

A horse feels the loss of his winter coat very considerably, so do not allow him to become chilled. Rug him up warmly and keep a set of wool bandages on his legs in the stable.

CARE OF MANE AND TAIL

The mane should hang over on the off side and be neatly pulled to about five inches in length. If it is the right length, but too thick, thin it by pulling from the under side which lies against the neck.

With the trimming scissors cut out the section of hair which lies under the head-piece of the bridle. The forelock should also be pulled to about five inches in length.

Thin the tail from the top to about nine inches down the dock. The majority of the hair should be pulled from the sides where it starts to grow. A tail with a full skirt looks best if it is cut straight across the bottom so that it hangs level with the point of the hocks when the horse is in motion. The tail will be carried higher when the horse is moving, so allow for this by cutting it off four inches below the point of the hocks when he is standing still. Cut the bottom of the tail off at a sloping angle so that it will hang level when the horse is in motion. Do this by cutting the hair which hangs furthest from the hocks about two inches longer than that which lies nearest to them. The exact difference in length must be determined by the individual tail carriage of each horse.

A tail with a thin skirt will look better if it is left uncut at the bottom.

To shape the tail, damp the hair on the dock with a water brush and keep a tail bandage on in the stable. Never wet the bandage or it may blister the skin on the nuder surface of the dock. Put the bandage on firmly and do not tie the tapes too tightly. Tapes on all bandages must be spread out flat before they are applied, otherwise they are likely to stop the circulation or cause discomfort.

HOW OFTEN TO CLIP

No hard-and-fast rule can be laid down for this because some horses grow their coats faster than others. It will keep the appearance smart and save a good deal of extra work in strapping if a horse is re-clipped whenever the coat has grown half an inch. This will be about every fortnight or three weeks before Christmas and once a month after.

When the winter coat starts to come out do not clip the horse again or it may spoil the appearance of the summer coat.

Good clipping and trimming is an art, but with a little practice it can be mastered by anyone who will continue to work slowly and carefully until they become proficient.

Hand-driven clipping machines are virtually things of the past and have been replaced by the electrical variety. An important point to remember when using electric clippers is that the connection to the power should be made to a 3-pin, earthed socket by means of the appropriate plug. It can be dangerous to make haphazard connections to a light fixture. The 'leg' knives, referred to in the text, comprise a pair of blades the teeth of which are set further apart to give a less close cut. They are, therefore, entirely suitable for trimming legs growing a lot of coarse hair without removing the growth entirely. Ed.

12

Difficult to Clip

N OTHING looks worse than a badly clipped horse, but it is almost impossible to make a good job of clipping if an animal is in an active state of rebellion throughout the entire operation. A skilled clipper and trimmer will only occasionally resort to mechanical aids to force a horse to submit, so do not fly for the twitch at the first sign of resentment; it is seldom necessary.

If a horse is difficult to clip, study his behaviour and try to find out the reason for his resentment, which will usually be found in one of the following causes:

1. *Nervousness.* A usual reaction when a horse is clipped for the first time.
2. *Fear.* Caused by rough handling or being nipped or cut by the knife on a previous occasion.
3. *Ticklishness.* Often found in Thoroughbreds, or in any horse with a thin, sensitive skin.
4. *Bad temper.* Seldom the cause, unless a horse is habitually bad-tempered in the stable.

NERVOUSNESS

It is usual for a horse to be nervous the first time he is clipped, especially if he is young. His future reaction to clipping will, to a great extent, depend on how he is handled the first time;

an unfortunate experience then may make him permanently difficult to clip.

First accustom him to the machine by allowing him to have a good look at it and smell it. When he has lost his fear, move it a few yards away from him and set it in motion. If he is nervous speak to him and make much of him. Before commencing to clip draw the stationary knife backwards down his neck and shoulder, but do not set it going until he is used to it. Then repeat the process when the knife is in motion, but do not start to clip before he is thoroughly accustomed to the feel of the blades moving against his skin.

Start on the shoulder and work up the neck. This is not a sensitive part of the body, so the horse is not likely to show resentment. If he becomes uneasy as the knife approaches his head, leave this part until later and continue over the front of the neck and breast.

Clip the top surface of the body first. This will allow the horse to become thoroughly used to the feel of the knife before tackling the more sensitive parts—under the belly, behind the elbow and the flank. When clipping these parts special care should be taken not to press the front edge of the knife into the skin or prod him with the corners.

If he shows nervousness or resentment speak to him quietly and firmly. A familiar voice, used in a way he understands, has great power to quieten some horses. When clipping behind the elbow an assistant should pull the horse's leg forward. A leg should also be held up if there is any trouble over clipping under the belly and flank. If the assistant places his hand under the front of the hoof it will prevent the horse leaning his weight on him, thereby making it more difficult for him to kick.

When clipping the hind quarters the operator should hold the horse's tail in his free hand. If the animal kicks the operator can then throw him off balance by pulling on it. If the horse will not settle down and stand quietly, put a blinker bridle on him; this often has the desired effect.

Most horses dislike having their head clipped, so leave it

F

until last, as it is pointless to put him in a bad humour by doing it first. The resentment a horse shows over having his head clipped is probably caused by the noise of the knife. No doubt the bones of the skull conduct and amplify the sound, and to a horse's sensitive hearing the noise in his head may be tremendous. Do not lose your temper with him if he turns rough. Give him a few minutes' rest, and before starting again the assistant should take a firm hold of his ear as close to the base as possible; this will deaden the sound and help to control the horse. On no account should the ear be twisted or deliberately hurt. If still more control is necessary the assistant must grasp the top lip with his other hand. A man with a strong grip can often anchor a restive horse in this way, and it will avoid the necessity of using a twitch. Give the horse a rest at intervals, and try not to stretch his endurance to breaking point.

FEAR

Once a horse has learned to connect clipping with pain he will naturally try to defend himself against what he regards as a painful operation. Rough handling and shouting will only make matters worse and do nothing to reassure him.

Follow the suggestions already given for a nervous horse. In addition try to take his mind off what is going on by giving him a handful of oats or a slice of carrot from time to time. It will take a great deal of time and patience to eradicate the horse's fear of being clipped, but with understanding and firm handling it can be done, providing he is not subjected to further pain. Improvement may be slow, but each time he is clipped he should be easier to do.

TICKLISHNESS

Many horses are exceptionally thin-skinned and ticklish, and Thoroughbreds are more prone to this trouble than other breeds. To this type of animal the feel of the moving knife against his skin is intolerable. Often he will cringe away from it until he loses his foothold, and in so doing may easily fall on the operator. It may be impossible to clip many parts of the body owing to the incessant twitching of the skin. A horse of this type which is normally quiet to handle often becomes violent and dangerous if forcibly restrained, and he will usually sweat so much that the knife will not cut.

The best and most humane way to deal with a horse of this kind is to consult your veterinary surgeon; explain the case, and ask him to prescribe a sedative which can be given in the feed an hour or so before clipping. This will deaden the nerves and the horse can then usually be clipped without any trouble.

BAD TEMPER

A horse which is normally bad-tempered in the stable is invariably an awkward customer to clip.

Do not confuse a bad-tempered horse with one that has acquired the unpleasant habit of nipping and 'slinging' a leg. This is not prompted by a deliberate intention to harm anyone. A vicious horse will aim at the person he means to kick, likewise he does not nip but takes a strong hold with his teeth and retains it. A bad horse will shake his victim, often striking at him at the same time.

Few people come in contact with horses of this nature. They are dangerous and require skilled handling. However, if one has to be clipped he must be forcibly controlled. Persuasion is useless, and will only increase the danger to those handling him, but this does not mean that the horse should be unnecessarily knocked about.

Put a pair of kneecaps on him to avoid possible damage to his knees. Then blindfold him. (As described under 'Blindfold'.) Next tie him up short to a ring about six foot from the ground. This may be enough to make him stand quietly, because many horses feel powerless once they are blindfolded. If this is not the case, strap up the foreleg on the side to be clipped first. Use a strap made for the purpose which goes round the forearm and then round the cannon bone, and is padded to prevent damage to the leg. If further restraint is necessary use a Comanche twitch. (As shown on Fig. 7, and explained under that heading.) This is more humane than an ordinary twitch because pressure need only be applied when the horse plays up. Even with a foreleg strapped up some horses can still kick viciously. A rap on the offending leg with a besom made of well-packed gorse may stop him.

If an ordinary twitch is used do not strap it to the head collar. This is a bad practice because the tension cannot be eased off when the horse is quiet. It should be held by an assistant and slackened whenever possible. If a twitch is left on too long or the pressure is too great it may permanently damage the nerves of the lip and cause paralysis, or a constant twitching. In either case it will spoil the horse's appearance. *Never* use a twitch on an ear; this may crush the muscles at the base, and damage the normal carriage of the ear.

In very few cases will all these methods of control be necessary, and much can be accomplished by common sense and tactful handling.

TO MAKE A BLINDFOLD

Stitch a double thickness of blanket to the browband of a head collar. It should be deep enough to hang several inches below the level of the eyes, and long enough to reach the bottom of the jaw on either side. Shape the blanket to lie flat under the cheek-pieces of the head collar. Attach tapes to all four corners and tie the top two under the throat, and the bottom two under the jaw.

COMANCHE TWITCH

Fasten a length of strong pliable cord, about the thickness of a man's finger, to the top 'D' on the near side of the head collar. Pass it over the poll and down the off-side cheek, then pass it under the top lip, so that it lies on the gum above the teeth. From there up the near-side cheek back to the 'D' where the other end is fastened. Pass it through the back of the 'D'

7. Comanche twitch

outwards, and leave about two feet of cord hanging loose. To restrain the horse pull on this cord until it bites into his gum, but do not use more pressure than is necessary to quieten him, and slacken it whenever possible.

TO MAKE AN ORDINARY TWITCH

For the handle cut eighteen inches off an old broom stale. Over the top of one end bind a piece of soft strong cord to form a loop four and a half inches long. The ends of the cord forming the loop must be placed opposite each other on either side of the handle, and bound firmly in position.

To apply the twitch slip the loop over the horse's top lip and twist the handle until the cord tightens. It should be just tight enough to keep the horse quiet and no more.

Do not bear a grudge against a vicious horse; remember he has to endure many unpleasant things for your pleasure and benefit, so *forget your own troubles and think of his.*

13

Difficult to Load

Few things can be more exasperating or a greater waste of time than a horse which habitually refuses to enter a horse box. The infuriated owner cannot be blamed if he comes to the conclusion that the 'brute' is plain stubborn and sets about him with a hunting whip. This method may have the desired result, but it will not lessen the horse's dislike of being loaded. Neither is it without danger to man and horse, and it requires more than one person to box the animal.

The working of a horse's mind is not easy to understand but, in my opinion, fear rather than stubbornness is at the root of the trouble. It may not be generally realized how many horses suffer from claustrophobia and are terrified when forced to enter a confined space. The hollow and unfamiliar sound of his feet on the ramp and floor of the box upsets some horses. To him it is probably a warning that the surface will not bear his weight. In this case the application of a whip accompanied by shouting and arm-waving will do nothing to improve his confidence.

How then, you may ask, is the animal to be loaded?

My method takes time and trouble, but it usually produces a permanent cure.

If you do not own a horse box you will have to borrow one, which can stand in your yard for at least three weeks. Straw the ramp and interior of the box well in order to muffle the hollow sound of the horse's feet.

In the evening water the horse at the usual time, then withhold all water until the following day. Before the morning feed put a head collar on him and lead him out with a head rope. Place a bucket of water a few yards up the ramp of the horse box so that he will have to put his feet on it to drink. Splash the water with your hand to make sure he knows it is there, then wait for him to mount the ramp of his own accord. Do not try to force him in any way. If he refuses to drink take him back to the stable and feed him, but do not water him. Follow the same procedure at each feed time until the horse will walk on to the ramp to drink. It will not be long before thirst overcomes his fear of stepping on the ramp. Continue to water him in this way until he steps on to the ramp as a matter of course. Then move the bucket so that he has to stand on the ramp with all four feet in order to drink. When he is accustomed to this, place the bucket at the front of the horse box, making sure that he knows where it is, and wait until he will enter the box of his own accord to drink. Once he will enter the box without hesitation feed him there as well.

Some horses load quite easily but become violent as soon as they are tied up. This aversion to being tied up is often difficult to cure, but it can sometimes be overcome by stabling the horse in the box until he is thoroughly accustomed to it. Do not tie him up in it for several days, and then do it quietly while he is feeding. Use a strong head collar and rope which will not break, because if he once breaks free it will be almost impossible to stop him trying to do so again. Bind the head-piece with something soft to prevent it from bruising or galling the skin if he pulls back and fights against the head rope. For this method the horse box must be strong and well built.

Some horses are bad travellers and always sweat on a journey. This may be caused by the anticipation of hunting, racing or showing which is usually preceded by a journey. To prevent this take the horse on short journeys which end in the yard where there is no excitement. Another cause of sweating may be travel-sickness due to the movement of the box. This can sometimes be prevented by turning the horse round, as some animals travel better facing the way they are going, and others in the reverse direction.

A horse seldom gives trouble without cause, and once this is discovered the cure is usually simple. They vary in temperament and behaviour as much as people and to get the best result each horse should be studied as an individual. Remember he is often a frightened and confused animal, but seldom a 'stubborn brute'.

For horses that 'break out' when travelling the provision of a cellular anti-sweat sheet, acting as an insulator when worn under a light sheet, will go a long way towards solving the problem. Ed.

14

The Shy Feeder

In the words of an old stableman a shy feeder is a 'proper headache', and sooner or later any owner who frequently changes his horses may find he has acquired one. If a veterinary surgeon can find no reason for a horse's lack of appetite it is then up to the owner to solve the problem himself.

Any breed of horse may be a shy feeder, but the majority are Thoroughbred with a highly strung irritable temperament. Study the horse's habits carefully and note the following points:

1. Does he eat better at night than at any other time?
2. Does any noise worry him, or only unusual sounds?
3. Does he eat better if the top half of the stable door is shut?
4. Is he encouraged to eat if he can hear another horse feeding?
5. Would he be more content if he had the company of another animal—cat or goat?

The shy feeder is a law unto himself and a clue to his precarious appetite may be found in any of the points I have mentioned. If not other possibilities will have to be explored. Keep him out of the stable for as many hours as possible each day, either at walking exercise or at grass. If the horse is clipped put a New Zealand rug on him before turning him out to graze for a few hours. This may relax his nerves so that he will settle down and feed when he comes in. Horses are creatures of habit and once he starts to feed normally he will probably continue to do so if he is gradually brought back to a normal routine.

Lack of appetite is sometimes caused by an irregularity of the kidneys, or acidity of the stomach. This may be put right by adding a lump of washing soda the size of a walnut to the drinking water every other day.

Try the effect of withholding all food from the horse for twenty-four hours, then give him a small bran mash and a little good hay. Clean the manger out and remove the hay net as soon as he appears to have had enough. Hunger will stimulate his desire for food, but the sight of it always before him will sicken him. If he will clean up even a very small feed there is every chance that he will continue to clean up when the amount is gradually increased.

It will be a great help if you can find something the horse particularly likes, and any of the following things may provide a solution:

1. Condition powders—try all brands.
2. A small handful of salt sprinkled on top of the feed.
3. Moist brown sugar, also sprinkled on top of the feed.
4. Carrots—pulped or sliced lengthways.
5. Flaked maize, porridge oats or any other cereal, stale bread and sliced apple. Any of these can be sprinkled on or mixed with the feed.

Aconite powders are well worthy trying; they are an excellent tonic, and much appreciated by some horses.

It is a good idea to place a small freshly cut sod of grass in the manger, roots uppermost. Put a small feed on top of this, and the horse may eat the lot. The soil will do him no harm and may provide something which his system lacks. If he enjoys a sod of grass give him one once or twice a week.

Some horses like their food dry, others prefer it damped.

A change can be introduced by damping feeds with one of the following: stewed linseed, black treacle and water, honey and water or old ale. If the horse is in very poor condition a gallon of milk and half a dozen eggs a day will help keep his strength up.

When lack of appetite cannot be traced to any organic cause, then the trouble is usually psychological. An indication of overstrained nerves may take the form of restlessness, box-walking or weaving, and in some cases the horse will stand motionless for hours, just staring into space and apparently seeing nothing. A mild sedative may prove beneficial, but the company of another horse is more likely to provide a solution. A horse which has always been used to the companionship of others will sometimes fret and go off his feed when he is deprived of company.

Mental anxiety may cause a horse to refuse his food, so handle him quietly and do everything possible to make him feel happy and content in himself.

15

An Eye for a Horse

W<small>HAT</small> is an 'eye for a horse'? It is often thought to be a mysterious gift, born in some people, but certainly not in the majority. Nothing could be further from the truth, because, with practice, anyone can acquire an eye for a horse, but naturally some people will become better judges than others.

The surest way to train your eye is to take advantage of every opportunity to study the conformation of horses, and especially good ones. In this way we begin to form a mental picture of what a well-constructed horse looks like. But first you must know why certain points are considered good and others bad. A horse must be judged on his suitability to perform the kind of work for which he is intended without undue strain, so that he will remain sound over a number of years.

Whenever you look at a horse you should carry in your mind an imaginary 'marking chart', and allocate a certain number of marks to the points I am going to list.

1. *Carriage* and *Presence*   10
2. *Balance*   10
3. *General Conformation* and *Appearance*   40
4. *Neck* and *Head*   10
5. *Shoulder, Forelegs* and *Feet*   30
6. *Back, Loins* and *Body*   10
7. *Quarters, Hind Legs* and *Feet*   30
8. *Action*   20

    9. *Ride*   20

   10. *Manners*   20

                                  ———

                        Total   200

As you will see I have divided the horse into ten sections, and allocated a maximum number of marks to each, making a possible total of 200.

Now let us go over these sections and see how we are going to form an opinion on the different points. I shall assume that the horse we are going to study is a hunter.

CARRIAGE AND PRESENCE

If a horse has this quality he will catch your eye right away by his bold and graceful bearing, vigour and personality. Coming towards you he will 'meet you well', and as he passes he will seem to be saying to himself, 'I'm *it*, so have a good look at me.' All good horses have carriage and presence, but unfortunately so do many bad ones; more especially thoroughbred 'weeds', which often catch the eye and are known as 'flat catchers'.

BALANCE

This means that the horse's weight is correctly distributed at every pace. In other words, that his centre of gravity is always so placed that whatever the position of his body he can make full use of his limbs at a moment's notice with the minimum of strain. Many falls are due to lack of natural balance. It is an easy quality to detect, because it is evident at all paces, and even when the horse is standing still.

GENERAL CONFORMATION AND APPEARANCE

These are the two contributing factors which make a show judge decide which horse he will call in first.

8. A horse with carriage and presence

Before you can become a good judge of a horse in action you must first learn to judge him when he is standing still. Study him methodically, starting at the head. Stand well back from him and study first one side, then the other. Try to form an opinion on the following points, and allocate your marks accordingly, bearing in mind that forty is the maximum for this section.

(a) Has he a good head, pleasing, well set on and in proportion to his body?
(b) Is his neck strong and supple; slightly arched at the crest, and straight on the under line?

95

(c) Has he a deep sloping shoulder; lean and muscular?

(d) Is his back strong and straight, with broad powerful loins; the whole neither too long nor too short?

(e) Are his quarters wide, deep, symmetrical and well packed with muscle?

(f) Are his hocks well placed to carry the weight of his quarters and broad and deep with clearly defined bone structure?

(g) Has he well-sprung ribs, with plenty of depth through the girth to allow sufficient space for heart and lungs?

(h) Is the under line of his body almost level, or does he run up in the flank and look 'herring-gutted'?

(i) Is his foreleg placed well forward, almost under the point of the shoulder? Does it appear clean-cut, strong and muscular?

(j) Does he show too much daylight under him?

(k) Are his feet well shaped with good horn texture, and in proportion to his body?

When you have carefully noted all these points, stand in front of the horse and study the conformation of his breast and forelegs.

(a) Is his breast reasonably wide, with prominent and well-developed muscles above the forelegs?

(b) Are the forelegs well spaced, straight and the knees big and bold?

(c) Does he stand level on his feet? Are they straight with no tendency to turn in or out? Are they well shaped and equal in size?

Now move to the rear.

(a) Are his hips wide, well placed and level?

(b) Are his hocks straight, large and clean-cut with no tendency to turn in or out?

(c) Are the quarters powerful, with well-developed cheeks, or does the horse appear 'split up', showing a lot of daylight between the legs at the top?

(d) Is his tail properly set on and carried well?

Next ask yourself, 'Has this horse quality?' Quality is not easy to define, but no successful show horse is ever without it. It does not always go with good breeding; a horse may have a wonderful pedigree, and yet be completely devoid of quality. It can best be described as all-round good conformation combined with power, natural balance and symmetry.

HEAD AND NECK

A horse's head must always be judged in relation to his body. It should be in proportion to his size and suitable for his type. There is a considerable difference in the heads of Thoroughbred horses, but they should always give the impression of quality —lean, clean-cut, prominent bone structure with the veins near the surface of the skin. A half- or three-quarter-bred horse should have an intelligent head, but a little lack of quality is permissible.

Ears should be of medium size and fine in texture. They often indicate temperament. Big ears usually denote a quiet placid nature, but beware of the horse with short, sharp ears set close together which nearly meet when they are pricked; in most cases his temper will be unpredictable. Lop-ears are ugly but the horse that has them is usually dependable and honest.

Eyes also give some indication of character. Look for a dark, bold eye, wide open and with a kind expression. Avoid a horse with a perpetually startled look; he will probably be nervous, impetuous or hot-headed. Small sunken eyes show a sullen, sulky temper, and the horse with a hard glassy stare which seems to focus on nothing is usually a 'queer customer'.

G

The muzzle should taper slightly and the lips close firmly. Full, open nostrils allow a free passage for air.

The head ought to be lightly and gracefully set on to the neck and give the impression that it can be easily flexed at the poll. If the neck is thick and heavy between the poll and gullet it will have little natural flexion. It is believed that horses with this conformation are liable to go wrong in the wind, and are also likely to be hard pullers. The opposite conformation is equally undesirable, and is known as 'cock-throttled', and it sometimes indicates a poor constitution.

The length of the neck should be in proportion to the body. A short stride is often found in a horse with a short neck and vice versa. The top line should be slightly arched and the under line straight. Viewed from the top the neck should look broad and strong, with the muscles on either side of the mane well developed. The neck muscles aid the movements of the shoulders, so if they are weak the horse will not use his shoulders to the best advantage.

A ewe neck is one shaped in the same way as a sheep's— dipped on the top line and convex on the bottom. A horse with this formation is often a 'star gazer' and difficult to control.

The neck should merge gradually into the shoulder and wither, with no marked dividing line between them.

SHOULDER, FORELEGS AND FEET

The shoulder is mainly comprised of the blade bone which runs from a point a few inches below the wither to the joint at the point of the shoulder. At the top it is held in position entirely by muscles. This blade bone should be well sloped in order to deflect the jar caused by the foot meeting the ground. If the shoulder is straight and upright the concussion of every step will be transmitted direct to the rider. A well-defined wither is an advantage because it prevents the saddle moving forward. The bone structure of the shoulder should be well defined, and the whole area appear lean and muscular. A fleshy, overloaded shoulder is seldom flexible and therefore incapable of fully extending the forearm.

Viewed from the side the foreleg should look strong and clean cut. The forearm broad, long and muscular, with the front line almost directly below the point of the shoulder, and the space between as short as possible. The knee must be large and bony and the front line slightly convex. On no account should this line be concave; a formation known as 'calf knee' or 'back at the knee', which throws undue strain on the back tendons. Look for a short cannon bone with the tendons at the back clearly defined beneath the skin. The back and front line of the leg below the knee should be parallel; not narrow at the top and wide above the fetlock. This formation affords weak attachments at the upper ends of the tendons and suspensory ligament, and renders them likely to break down under strain.

Viewed from the side, the fetlock joint should appear broad and flat; this indicates strong attachments at the lower end of the tendons and suspensory ligament. These indications are lacking in a small round joint which is a frequent source of unsoundness. From the knee to the fetlock is the weakest part of the foreleg, so pay special attention to the points which indicate strength. These are—a short cannon bone, good measurement and breadth below the knee and above the fetlock, strong clean-cut back tendons which show up well.

The pastern should slope at an angle of approximately forty-five degrees to the ground, be of medium length and appear sturdy enough to bear the weight above. An upright pastern does not absorb the concussion of the foot meeting the ground, so jars the entire limb and makes the horse an uncomfortable ride.

Always pay special attention to the shape and conformation of the forefeet. No matter how good a horse may be in other respects he will be virtually useless if his feet are weak and unserviceable. They should be in proportion to the size of the animal and must match each other in size and shape, have strong smooth horn and a well-developed frog. A small foot gives insufficient bearing surface and cramps the interior structure. A large, flat foot is even more undesirable. The toe is usually too long and the heel so low that the coronet almost comes to the ground at the back. This type of foot invariably produces poor-quality horn, and this coupled with the almost horizontal slope of the walls affords an insecure nail hold. The sole is usually flat, thin and liable to constant bruising.

Make a special study of good feet, and then compare them with feet which are weak. Never forget the truth of the old saying, '*No foot, no horse*'.

BACK, LOINS AND BODY

The weight of the rider is carried midway between the fore- and hind limbs, with no support directly beneath it. Therefore, it is not difficult to understand why the back must be short and strong, and the loin broad and muscular, rising slightly towards the quarters. This slight rise gives strength to the back in much the same way as an arch gives strength to a bridge. A long back and weak loin cannot bear a heavy weight without risk of strain. A little extra length is permissible in a mare to provide space in the body for the development of a foal. The back carries the saddle and should be level, but the slight rise over the loin denotes strength and is desirable, especially in a jumper. However, a *pronounced* upward curve over the loin is a mal-formation, termed 'roach back', which is akin to curvature of the spine and prevents a horse from fully extending himself.

A hollow back is a weakness and a serious defect in a young horse, likely to become more pronounced with age. An old horse with many years of dressage behind him usually develops a slightly hollow back owing to the nature of his work, but this should not be regarded as a serious fault.

The ribs should be well sprung, and the body have depth and substance, especially through the girth. This allows room for the heart and plenty of space for the lungs to expand. A horse that runs up in the flank is often a bad doer with a weak constitution, and is described as 'herring-gutted' or 'wasp-waisted'.

QUARTERS, HIND LEGS AND FEET

In outline the quarters should be powerful and symmetrical, with hips spaced well apart. Excessive width sometimes gives a ragged angular appearance; this is not detrimental to a working hunter, but is usually frowned upon by show judges.

The croup extends from the high bone formation behind the loins to the root of the tail and should slope gently. When this line drops sharply the horse is said to have a 'goose rump'. The opposite extreme is known as 'flat-quartered'. Both these formations spoil a horse for show, but do not detract from his usefulness.

The top area of the hind quarter which lies between the point of the hip and the buttock and extends down to the stifle should be shaped like a pear, base uppermost. It must be wide, covered with well-developed muscle, and closely knit into the body. The muscles in this area provide most of the power which both lifts and propels the horse forward. The leg between the stifle and the hock is called the second thigh or gaskin and it must be broad and packed with muscle. Strength here is particularly desirable in a jumper.

The hock is also closely connected with impulsion, so it must be bold and strong. Viewed from the side it should have plenty of width and rest squarely on the cannon bone beneath. The whole joint should appear big, bony and clean-cut. Small fleshy hocks are usually weak and subject to strain and unsoundness.

Below the hock the cannon bone should drop in a straight line to the fetlock, and be placed so that it can best bear the weight of the quarters. When the horse is standing squarely on his hind legs a perpendicular line dropped from the point of the buttock to the ground should touch the point of the hock and the back of the fetlock. If the natural position of the leg extends behind this imaginary line, then the horse is said to have his hocks 'away from him', or in dealers' jargon 'in the next county'. When the reverse is the case and the hocks appear permanently bent, it is termed 'sickle hock'. Both these formations are a weakness as the hocks will not be placed in the best position to carry weight and will be subject to unnecessary strain.

The hock should be well 'let down' and closely knit into a short strong cannon bone. Viewed from the side the line from the point of the hock to the fetlock must be straight, with no tendency to curve outwards at the back of the hock where it merges into the cannon bone. An outward curve at this point is a 'curb' which will render the horse unfit to carry a heavy weight, and is especially detrimental to a hunter or jumper. The front line of the cannon bone and the back line of the tendons should run parallel down to the fetlock. The hind fetlock and pastern should have the same conformation as that previously described for the forelegs.

The walls of the hind feet are far more upright than those of the forefeet, and are therefore stronger and less liable to suffer from defects common in the forefeet. They should be well proportioned, have good texture, sound horn and be wide enough at the heel to allow the frog to develop fully.

From the rear the quarters should look wide and powerful, with level hips, and muscles well defined from the point of the hip to hock. The distance between these two points cannot be too long or the hock placed too low. The inside and outside lines of both hocks must be alike, and the joints should look as if they are a matched pair. The points must be level and neither turn inwards or outwards. Hocks which turn towards each other are described as 'cow hocks'.

The muscles inside the tops of the legs (cheeks of the buttocks) should be well developed and almost touching. A 'split-up' appearance which gives a view along the under line of the belly is not desirable.

A well-set-on tail improves the appearance, and it should be gaily carried. In a Thoroughbred horse the dock should be fairly thin and the hair soft and silky.

ACTION

A good action implies that the horse moves freely and lightly, with perfect balance, and without obvious effort. The usual paces are the walk, trot, canter and gallop. Of these the first and last are the most natural. If you watch a bunch of young horses at grass, you will notice that they invariably walk or gallop, and seldom trot or canter for more than a short distance.

A great deal may be learned from the way a horse walks, because it is the foundation of all other paces. The stride should be long, low and vigorous; comparatively effortless, and yet bring into play almost every bone and muscle in the body —in other words, the horse should 'use himself' as he walks. The forefeet should touch the ground lightly with spring and resilience, which reduces the effort required for the next step. The foot should move close to the ground with as little knee action as possible. Watch how the horse places his feet. If the hind foot is placed well in advance of the imprint of the forefoot he will usually have speed and gallop well. Stand behind him as he walks away from you and notice if the limbs move in a straight line, without any tendency to swing the feet outwards or inwards. The legs should not move too close together or there will be the danger of one foot striking the opposite leg. This is a serious fault; always difficult and often impossible to cure. If a horse swings his tail in a wide sweep from side to side as he walks he will usually gallop well.

The trot should be light and swinging, with low knee action, rhythm and balance. The feet must move in a straight line and not be thrown out to the side—this is called 'dishing'. It is not a serious fault in a hunter, but will spoil a horse for show.

The canter is a somewhat artificial gait, and how well the

horse moves will depend to some extent on his schooling. In common with all other paces it must be light and smooth, and carried out with rhythm and balance.

A horse that gallops well will seem to sweep over the ground with a long low stride; his body will appear to stretch out and flatten as he reaches for the ground ahead, and with effortless ease he will use every ounce of his muscular strength.

RIDE AND MANNERS

I will not try to describe these, because every horseman has his own personal preference and opinion concerning both qualities.

A horse of bad conformation is never a good ride, and one devoid of manners is not likely to appeal to anyone.

JUDGING A HORSE IN THE ROUGH

This is always difficult, because it is essential that you must be able to judge the horse not as he is, but as he will be when he is fit and muscled up. In the rough many of his muscles are soft and undeveloped through lack of work. They may also be hidden under a heavy coat, and possibly too much flesh. However, providing he is fully grown his frame will not alter, and on this you must base your judgement. The body should be in good proportion and well balanced. The legs must look and feel hard and clean, with bold well-developed joints. If there is a fair growth of hair on his legs feel beneath it for the underlying conformation.

Make sure he is a straight mover without pronounced knee action, but remember that an excited horse 'high-tailing' round a field will always show an exaggerated knee action. If he is over-fat he may 'roll' a little, but this should disappear when he becomes fitter.

It is easy to judge the bone structure of a thin horse, but what his ultimate shape will be will depend on where he puts on flesh and develops muscle. Even an experienced judge may find a horse turns out very different to what he expected. All thin horses look a bit lengthy, but will seem much more compact when they have muscled up and put on flesh over the loins and quarters.

A sprawling action is often caused by weakness, and should not be judged too harshly providing the horse is a straight mover.

The feet may be overgrown and ragged, but if the horn is sound and they are well shaped this can be put right by a blacksmith.

NO HORSE IS PERFECT

It takes years of experience to become a good judge of a horse, so never miss an opportunity to study *good* horses, both in the flesh and from photographs, in this way the right conformation will become fixed in your mind. Only then should you make a study of bad horses in order to compare them.

Every judge has a personal preference for one type of horse rather than another. Good horses vary considerably in type, so no judge should allow himself to become too biased on this point.

If you are tempted to award any horse the maximum number of marks remember that the perfect horse has not yet been foaled, so your judgement must be at fault somewhere. Likewise, no horse is without some redeeming features. If you cannot discover them go back to his head and go over him again point by point. It is only by constantly studying shape, proportion, balance and action that you will develop *an eye for a horse*.

16

Description of Horses for Sale

W HETHER you are buying a horse at a sale or through an advertisement it is essential to carefully study the wording of the description. If certain words are used to describe a horse they are recognized in law as giving or implying a warranty. If the horse does not merit the warranty it is sold with, then it can be returned by the purchaser within one week of the date of sale, and the purchase price and expense incurred reclaimed.

Conditions of Sale, and certain descriptions which imply a warranty, are printed on the back of every sale catalogue and should be carefully read. Pay special attention to rules which apply to horses sold under a stated price. These rules are binding, and if the purchaser has not complied with them he will have no redress.

If an owner has a good genuine horse for sale he will usually give a description which covers the main essentials, and is clear and to the point. The following is an example:

'Bay gelding, eight years, sixteen hands, two inches. By X, dam by Y. A good hunter. Brilliant performer over any country. A hard horse that can stay and gallop. Snaffle mouth. Quiet to ride in all traffic. Free from vice. Easy to clip, shoe and box. Veterinary Certificate of Soundness.'

Now let us examine this description and see what the twelve points mean, and which of them imply a warranty.

1. *Colour and sex*
2. *Age*
3. *Height*
4. *Breeding.* If any of these points are incorrect the horse can be returned because it does not fulfil its description.
5. *A good hunter.* This is a warranty that the horse is sound in wind and eye, and capable of being hunted. But it does not necessarily imply that he will merit a Veterinary Certificate of Soundness. However, he must be sound enough to hunt, and can therefore be returned if he is lame. 'Capable of being hunted' also means that he has no confirmed vice which would make it impossible to hunt him. It does not imply that the horse is suitable for a novice rider.
6. *Brilliant performer over any country.* This warrants the horse to be a safe free jumper over a fair hunting country. If he proves to be a confirmed refuser when hounds are running he can be returned.
7. *Can gallop and stay.* This is not a warranty because no specified speed or distance is mentioned.
8. *Snaffle mouth.* This states that the horse can be hunted and controlled in a snaffle. It might be a difficult point to dispute, because much depends on the ability and strength of the rider.
9. *Quiet to ride in all traffic.* This is a definite guarantee that the horse is quiet in this respect.
10. *Free from vice.* This is a warranty to the effect that the horse is not nappy, and does not buck, kick, rear or bolt under normal circumstances, and is free from stable vices.
11. *Quiet to shoe, clip and box.* Is a warranty covering these points.
12. *Veterinary Certificate of Soundness.* This means that the horse has been examined by a veterinary surgeon and passed sound on the date the certificate was issued, and is available for the purchaser to see.

If you have bought a horse below a certain price (as stated in the Conditions of Sale) it will usually have to be examined before it leaves the sale yard, and cannot be returned for any defect after it has been removed. Conditions of Sale vary on this point and should be carefully studied.

If you buy a horse at a sale, and later find that it does not merit the description given in the catalogue, get in touch with the auctioneer at once. Tell him you are returning the horse, and state the reason. If the animal is not returned within the time specified in the Conditions of Sale your claim will not be valid.

Should the horse be unsound when you get him home, have him examined by your own veterinary surgeon before returning him to the sale yard. If he has been lamed in transit there would be no breach of warranty, so it would be useless to return him. If, however, your vet considers the unsoundness to be of long standing, then the auctioneer will have the horse re-examined by an independent veterinary surgeon whose decision will be final and binding.

If the matter in dispute concerns manners or performance, the auctioneer will appoint an independent arbitrator to try the horse, and his opinion and ruling must be accepted.

If you have bought a horse through an advertisement in a newspaper, and it does not comply with the description, write to the vendor without delay, expressing clearly and politely where you consider the description constitutes a breach of warranty. If he will not admit this, and refuses to take the horse back and refund the purchase price, place the matter in the hands of your solicitor and allow him to deal with it. If the vendor's reply to your first letter is unsatisfactory, do not personally enter into further correspondence with him. Should the matter come to court, your letter would probably be produced, and it might not weigh in your favour.

The following is an example of a glowing description which gives absolutely no warranty:

'Black hunter mare, fifteen hands, three inches. Young. Well bred. Good-looking. A spectacular performer. Ridden by a girl. Winner every time shown. Should have a great future. Reasonable price to good home.'

This advertisement means to convey the impression that the animal is a nice hunter mare. A good performer in the hunting field. A winner in the show ring with a bright future, and suitable for a girl to ride.

Now we will pull it to pieces and see just how little it really means.

1. *Black hunter mare, fifteen hands, three inches.* This tells us that the animal is black, a mare and fifteen hands, three inches. It is a statement of fact and can be taken as correct. The word 'hunter' by itself carries no warranty.

2. *Young.* Does not state any definite age, and could be a matter of opinion.

3. *Well bred.* This description without any mention of the mare's pedigree is worthless.

4. *Good-looking.* An ambiguous remark, implying nothing definite.

5. *A spectacular performer.* This could apply to an animal which falls on its face over every jump, or gives a rodeo performance every time it is mounted!

6. *Ridden by a girl.* The age of the girl is not mentioned, neither does it say if she rode the mare hacking, hunting, showing, or for a few paces while a strong man hung on to its head.

7. *Winner every time shown.* This statement could be proved, so it is probably true, but it does not mention where, or in what type of class the animal won. It could have been as a foal, or in hand between the age of one and three years old. If that was the case it might no longer be up to show standard.

8. *Should have a great future.* It would be interesting to know in what field!

9. *Reasonable price to good home.* This gives the impression that the mare is a 'family pet', and that the owner is willing to sacrifice a certain amount of cash in order to secure a good home for her. It does not actually say so, but the remark is calculated to attract an inexperienced buyer.

This animal might be unsound and unrideable, and if you bought her on the strength of the advertisement it is unlikely that you would be able to return her, because the description carries no warranty that she is either sound or quiet to ride.

In all descriptions look for statements which are clear, and cannot be misinterpreted. These usually give a warranty on the points to which they refer. If the animal does not merit it, and the case goes to court, then there is an excellent chance that the judge will find in your favour.

Never interpret a description into what you hope it means. The words 'sound', 'quiet', etc., are never omitted by mistake.

When buying a horse in a sale yard the following points are worth remembering:

If an owner sends up several horses for sale they are usually genuine animals and fairly described. Faults can sometimes be found by noting what points have *not* been mentioned.

Single horses often come under the hammer owing to some vice or unsoundness. This is by no means always the case, but extra care is needed when studying their description.

Beware of any horse which is described as 'The Property of a Gentleman', 'The Property of a Lady', or 'Sold to Dissolve a Partnership'. If an owner does not wish to put his or her name to a horse there is usually something wrong with it.

Avoid horses which constantly come up for sale. It is obvious that they have found no favour with their previous buyers. A groom belonging to the sale yard will usually be able to tell you which horses have been there before. Do not ask him a lot of searching questions; it is not his job to crab any horse sent up for sale.

An animal described as a 'gay or keen ride' is usually unsuitable for a novice, and a 'strong ride' is nearly always a puller.

If you are not accustomed to buying horses at a sale or through advertisements seek the advice of a knowledgeable friend, and be guided by his opinion. If you want to know if a horse is sound, have it examined by a veterinary surgeon.

With a little experience, and by keeping your eyes and ears open, you will soon be able to buy a horse on your own judgement, without making elementary mistakes.

Remember it is as important to have an '*eye for an advertisement*' as it is to have an '*eye for a horse*'.

17

Preparing a Plain Horse for Sale

A PLAIN HORSE may be a first-rate hunter, but unless this is widely known he may be difficult to sell.

With a little judicious use of a clipping knife, and by one or two other means, his weak points may be disguised and his general appearance considerably improved.

The best time to sell this type of horse is in the autumn, when it will be easier to produce him in the condition which shows him to the best advantage. Study the horse carefully, and decide if his appearance will be improved by plenty of flesh or the reverse. If he is normally proportioned he will look best in medium condition. A heavy-topped horse will show this defect less if he is hard and lean, and plenty of flesh will help to hide a weak neck and long back.

Clever trimming can improve a plain horse out of all recognition, but not much can be done to improve him if he is sold in the rough.

Taking one point at a time I will try to explain how an optical illusion can often be created.

A LARGE OR COARSE HEAD

Use the thinnest blades you can get, and clip the hair as close as possible, especially under the jaw and round the muzzle. Clip the ears inside as well as outside, and do not make the forelock too short or too thin.

PLAIN OR SLIGHTLY EWE NECK

Leave the mane fairly long and thick. Never hog it or put it up. Brush it over to the *near* side, so that the hair which normally lies underneath is on top. Saturate the roots and the hair for about two inches of its length with any preparation sold for stiffening and setting human hair. Allow this to dry, then gently turn the mane over to the off side, and brush it lightly down. The hair underneath which has been stiffened will rise above the natural line of the neck before falling over and this will do much to improve the top line of a weak neck. The solution should only be applied where it is necessary to bring the line of the neck up. Do not stiffen the hair which lies on top of the mane or its natural appearance will be spoiled.

STRAIGHT SHOULDER AND LONG BACK

Clip the saddle patch two or three inches further back than the place where the horse actually carries the saddle, and extend the back of the patch well towards the loin. This will give the illusion of lengthening his front and shortening his back.

NARROW QUARTERS

These will appear wider if the hair at the top of the tail is well thinned to about nine inches down. Shape with a tail bandage, and leave the skirt full. Well-placed water marks will also help to give an impression of width.

FORE- AND HIND-LEGS

If the forearm is narrow clip the top of the stocking in a straight line across, just below the elbow. Finish the hind stocking in the same way; clipping in a straight line across the leg about two inches below the stifle. This will make the legs look wider than they are, whereas a slanting line will have the opposite effect.

H

TIED IN BELOW THE KNEE

It will straighten the line down the back of the leg from the knee to the fetlock if the hair round the fetlock is clipped close. Taper the hair up the back of the leg so as to leave no hard finishing line.

FEET

A good blacksmith can vastly improve the appearance of weak feet, but in order to do this he may have to shoe the horse several times.

TO IMPROVE THE COAT

Damp one feed a day with a cupful of well-stewed linseed for about a month before the horse is to be sold. Strap regularly and wisp the horse for at least ten minutes each day.

EXERCISE

Plenty of fast walking and steady trotting up- and downhill will help to put muscle on in the right places, and this will improve the appearance of any horse.

School the horse to stand well on his legs, and run freely in hand.

The work and trouble required to turn a plain horse out looking his best is usually well repaid, and it is not a crime to show your horse looking his best!

18

Importance of Good Shoeing

A<small>T THE</small> beginning of this century the greater part of a blacksmith's earnings came from shoeing horses. As a boy he learned his trade under a good shoeing smith, and gained a wealth of experience by shoeing a variety of horses engaged in different types of work. Every agricultural show had its shoeing competitions, which were always well filled and the rivalry keen.

Today, shoeing provides an infinitesimal part of a blacksmith's income, and is always accompanied by the risk of injury which may put him out of work for weeks. Unless he intends to earn his entire living by shoeing horses, a boy cannot be blamed if he does not wish to undergo a long and poorly paid apprenticeship to learn the trade. Instead, he learns the bare essentials necessary to shoe the few horses which come his way.

The knowledge, skill and artistry required to make and fit a shoe perfectly is a closed book to many horse owners. With so little knowledge of a blacksmith's craft, they cannot differentiate between a poor workman and a skilled one. To help them to form a sound opinion of a blacksmith's work I will try to explain the difference between a good man at his job and a bad one.

A BAD BLACKSMITH

As soon as your horse is in his forge he will start to remove the shoes without first troubling to study the feet. When they are off they will be cast aside without a glance to see how or where the horse has worn them down. Without examining the foot first he will take a knife and cut down the overgrown wall, then, still using the knife, considerably reduce the thickness of the sole, and cut the frog to his liking. Next, a set of machine-made shoes of approximately the right size will be produced. Heating and burning them on as a matter of routine, he will pay scant attention to fitting them, apart from widening or narrowing the heels as he thinks fit. When he has nailed them on he will wring the ends off the nails and hammer down the clinches. This done, the foot will be vigorously rasped until it fits the shoe. A liberal coating of sump oil applied to the freshly rasped walls will complete the job. And now, sir, your horse is 'done'—probably in every sense of the word!

From this I do not mean to imply that all the blacksmiths today are all poor workmen. This is definitely not so; some of them could hold their own with the shoeing smiths of any age, but these are few and far between.

THE SKILLED SHOEING SMITH

A good blacksmith will carefully study a horse's feet, especially if he has not shod him before. He will note their general shape and condition, the texture of the horn, and if the forefeet are identical in shape, and also notice if the fetlocks are showing signs of wear. If he finds something abnormal he will question the owner about the horse's work and his action, and will probably have him run out in hand so that he can study it for himself. From this he can usually judge if the horse is favouring one side of the foot more than the other. If so he may thicken or lower one part of the shoe in order to distribute the weight more evenly. A slight adjustment of this kind can save the fetlock joint a great deal of unnecessary strain.

When he has removed the shoes he will examine them care-fully to find out just where the metal has had the most wear. He will use a knife and probably a buffer to trim the walls and bars of the feet, and then lightly rasp the foot straight across without reducing the thickness of the sole. He may trim off any ragged pieces on the frog, but will never cut it away so as to reduce its size.

A good blacksmith will only use machine-made shoes if the horse's feet are stock size, otherwise he will make a set of shoes to fit him. In either case he will take the greatest care over the fitting, and the feet will never be rasped down and made to fit the shoes. When burning the shoe on to the foot he will examine the mark it has left to see if the bearing of the shoe is level, and it will not be nailed on until he is satisfied that it is. When the clinches have been nailed down he will rasp them lightly, taking as little as possible off the surface of the walls. If the surface of the walls are constantly rasped the horn will soon become unhealthy. Finally the hoofs will be brushed over with a mixture of hoof oil and Stockholm Tar. And now, sir, your horse is *shod*.

SHOEING ACCIDENTS

If the wall of the hoof is thin, or the horn of poor quality, it will be extremely difficult for a blacksmith to nail a shoe on securely. While endeavouring to obtain a firm nail-hold, he may inadvertently drive the nail too close to the sensitive part of the foot. If the horse goes lame a day or two after he has been shod this will probably be the cause, so have the shoe removed and re-nailed.

Any blacksmith may prick the sensitive part of the foot if a horse suddenly snatches it away when he is driving in a nail, causing the hammer to deflect it from the intended course. These mishaps are often unavoidable, and are not necessarily due to lack of skill on the part of the blacksmith.

COLD SHOEING

Some owners have their horse shod in this way because it saves the time and trouble of taking them to a forge. At one time this method was only used to plate a horse before a race, and as the shoe was only left on for a short period it did no harm. In my opinion a horse should never be shod by this method if the shoes are intended for ordinary use, because, without the aid of heat in the shaping and fitting of a shoe, it is impossible to obtain a perfect fit and level bearing.

THE EFFECT OF BAD SHOEING

More unsoundness is caused directly and indirectly by bad shoeing than by any other single factor. The fine balance between the fetlock joint, the pastern bones and the inner structure of the foot can be thrown out of true by an ill-fitting shoe, thus causing abnormal strain on all the parts involved. The walls of the foot are growing all the time, and because they are fixed to the shoe they must follow its shape, whether it be good or bad. If you consider this point you will realize how easy it is for a blacksmith to improve or ruin the shape of a foot.

If you want your horse to remain sound and serviceable for many years never neglect his feet, and ensure that he is well shod at all times.

The author is quite correct in expressing a preference for 'hot' shoeing but it is a fact that many horses today have to be shod cold or not at all. If it is at all possible have your horse shod hot, if it is not, then you must console yourself with the knowledge that hundreds of horses are shod cold without coming to any great harm. Ed.

19

Loss of Nerve

Aᴏᴛᴇʀ a fall it is not uncommon for a horse to lose his nerve
to such an extent that he is afraid to jump even a small obstacle. Sometimes it is impossible to restore his confidence, but
this is seldom the case if he is handled with understanding and
common sense.

When a horse's nerve has been badly shaken by a fall,
never try to force him over a jump. This is likely to establish the
sense of fear in his mind and may turn him into a habitual
refuser, and probably a rearer as well. It is wiser to turn him
out to grass for a few months which will give him a chance to
forget the whole business. When he is brought up from grass
a spell of hunting may restore his confidence. First try him
over a low easy fence when hounds are running. If he takes this
in his stride you can carry on from there, taking great care not
to overface him or risk giving him another fall over a trappy
place.

Unfortunately it is not always so easy to restore a horse's
nerve. If he will not jump even when hounds are running
it is useless to persevere on these lines.

Riding him over cavalletti may help to improve his nerve.
If they are raised by imperceptible stages, you may in due
course find that he will jump a sizable fence without hesitation.
This method is often quite successful until the obstacles reach
about three feet, when the horse's lack of nerve may suddenly
return. If this happens you will have to try another plan.

Obtain permission from a riding school to hack the horse about in a field where ponies are being schooled over small jumps. If your horse appears worried by the sight of the ponies jumping, keep him well away from them until he settles down. Gradually bring him closer until he will stand by the jumps while the ponies are negotiating them. This may revive his fear so do not be in a hurry to force him too close to the jumps.

When he will stand quietly without any show of uneasiness, slip him in behind the last pony and let him follow it over a little fence. Ride the horse as if the fence wasn't there, and with as little fuss as possible. He will probably be on the other side before he has time to fear the consequence. If so, make much of him, but do not try to repeat the experiment again the same day. Continue in this way—never giving the horse time to anticipate a jump. Then, if he is not hurried, his confidence should gradually return. When it has he can be put over a variety of small jumps; always well within his ability, and with another horse to give him a lead.

If his progress is satisfactory a spell of hunting should increase his confidence. Never ask him to jump in cold blood, or without a lead from another horse, until his nerve is completely restored.

Each individual horse requires slightly different handling, and the key to success is time, patience and understanding, which in due course should help him to forget his fear. Avoid forceful tactics; they will only make matters worse.

When a fall is accompanied by considerable pain it is not to be wondered at if the horse's nerve goes, but once he finds he can negotiate a fence safely he will soon forget the unpleasant consequences of a previous fall.

20

Winter Care of a Horse at Grass

With the exception of Thoroughbreds most horses winter out well if they are properly fed.

Everything a horse eats is converted into units of heat. Roughly speaking, these are used up in three ways—to provide warmth and energy and to rebuild waste tissue. In summer good grazing will supply all a horse requires, and supplementary feeding is only necessary if he is in hard work. Grass begins to lose its value at the onset of winter and the first frosts; after that continuous rain and snow will further reduce its quality. Then if a horse is not given additional food he will soon become debilitated because he will not be getting enough heat units to supply his needs. Most of his food will be used to keep him warm and to provide energy for movement, so there will be little or nothing left to replace waste tissue or to retain a reasonable layer of fat.

This is when a horse's constitution will first begin to suffer, and his stomach and digestive organs will lose tone, which will lay him open to the ravages of internal parasites, particularly red worm. Next the blood will become poor, and this may bring on various types of skin trouble which will cause the coat to fall out in patches. A horse in very poor condition soon becomes a prey to lice which will further sap his strength.

When there is no fat to nourish the muscles they become weak and lose their resilience, and the horse will be subject to strains and sprains which would not normally occur.

Some owners do not worry if a horse gets a bit low in condition during the winter, because they think he will soon pick up when the new grass comes. This assumption is often correct, but, for all that, many horses die in the spring, because their constitution has been so undermined by the rigours of winter that they can no longer digest their food properly, and so derive no benefit from the spring grass. This is by no means an uncommon occurrence if the horse is heavily infested with red worm.

A horse at grass during the winter cannot be fed by rule of thumb; his needs will depend on the nature of the grazing, the severity of the weather and the horse's constitution and condition. Condition must always be your guide. Do not form an opinion by just looking at the animal—a heavy winter coat can successfully hide a rack of bones. Feel the tone of his muscles, and note if the skin is hidebound. Even if he is in light condition he may be perfectly healthy, but if he 'feels' wrong when you handle him you may be sure he is deteriorating.

It is not usually necessary to feed hay until the middle or end of October, but if the weather has been continuously wet before then it is advisable to feed a little hay, as it will help to keep the grass in the horse long enough for him to derive the full benefit from it.

When the addition of hay becomes necessary, start by giving five or six pounds of good hay once a day, and increase it gradually to twelve pounds, given in two feeds. When the weather becomes hard the horse will require concentrates in addition to hay. The following is a good mixture:

4 lb. crushed oats.	1 lb. broad bran.
3 lb. flaked maize.	1 lb. old split beans.
3 lb. chaff.	

Divide this into two feeds a day.

In mild weather this quantity may be reduced because the horse will not be using up so many units of heat to keep him warm.

At all times he should have a plentiful supply of good drinking water. Do not forget to break the ice on it at least twice a day in frosty weather.

It is a false economy to cut down on winter feeding, because the cost of getting a horse back into condition will be far greater than the amount saved.

A horse which looks well at the end of a winter at grass reflects great credit on the management and care he has rec eived.

The term 'hidebound' used on the facing page implies a dry, dull skin often giving the appearance of being stretched. Hidebound is not a disease but a condition. Usually it is accompanied by a harsh, 'staring' coat and is indicative of a heavy red-worm burden. Ed.

21

Additional Education for a Child's Pony

CHILDREN get themselves and their ponies into situations and predicaments undreamed of by the average adult, so the more 'shockproof' a pony is the safer it will be.

Children should be taught from the start to handle their ponies correctly and treat them with respect, but even so it is natural for them to learn most things by personal experience, and experience may be a hard school when the teacher is a frightened pony.

In addition to the usual training, a pony should be gradually accustomed to all manner of strange sights, sounds and happenings. I have stressed the word 'gradually' because nothing will be gained by frightening the pony half out of its wits by subjecting it to a succession of unusual occurrences.

By far the most important lesson is to teach the pony to stop without fail at the word 'Whoa'. This should be instilled into it from the start of its training. When first teaching it to lead in hand, say 'Whoa'—make it stop, and then reward it. Do the same on the lunge rein and in long reins, and throughout every stage of its training. If the pony will stop at a word of command it will save many minor mishaps and accidents, and may even save a child's life.

In my opinion all the following items should be included in the making and training of a child's pony:

A BRANCH TRAILING ON THE GROUND

Children often make little jumps out of hedge clippings, and if a pony gets a piece caught up in his tail he may become frightened and play merry hell, but if he is used to a branch trailing behind him he will take no notice.

Get an assistant to drag a branch while walking beside the pony. When it is accustomed to this, attach two small branches to the stirrup irons with a suitable length of rope, and let the pony drag them about. Gradually shorten the ropes until the branches are trailing close to his hocks.

HOB-NAILED BOOTS, ROLLER SKATES AND TIN CANS

The sound of any of these things rattling on the ground can frighten a pony to the point of bolting, but he will soon become accustomed to it if he is allowed to stand well away and see what is going on. When his nervousness subsides gradually bring him closer. Any of these 'horrors' may be encountered in a village street, so be sure he gets well used to them, also to a bouncing football.

A CHILD ON THE GROUND

Normally a pony sees a human being in an upright position, and is often frightened by the sight of a person sitting, lying or rolling on the ground, and for this reason may kick at a child who falls off. When an accident of this nature occurs it is usually because the pony is frightened by a happening not previously experienced and it should not be thought that its action is prompted by wickedness.

To lessen the possibility of such mishaps the trainer should accustom the pony to seeing someone on the ground near its legs. Start by sitting down in the stable and offering the pony a piece of carrot or sugar to gain its confidence. Once this is accomplished it will not be long before the trainer can sit, lie or roll close to the pony's legs without causing alarm. It should also be taught to stand quietly if someone ducks under its belly or slides off over its tail.

If a pony is accustomed to such happenings it will not be so likely to kick if a child falls off or gets dragged.

FLAPPING CLOTHES AND NEWSPAPERS

Children have a habit of putting their coats on or taking them off without dismounting, and unless a pony has been taught to disregard this sort of thing he may become frightened and cause an accident. He should also be accustomed to the sight of clothes flapping on a line, and sheets of newspaper blowing about.

UMBRELLAS, PRAMS AND DOGS

It is surprising how many people will suddenly open an umbrella or sunshade almost in a pony's face without realizing that it may frighten him. So accustom him to umbrellas being opened and shut at close quarters. He should also be taught to disregard a pram, and not to kick at it even if it touches his quarters.

Dogs are everywhere, so get the pony used to them running round his feet, barking and jumping up.

SUDDEN LOUD NOISES

If a pony is used to the sound of a shotgun going off at close quarters it will take no notice of cars backfiring, thunder or fireworks.

First let it hear the sound of a gun at a distance, then gradually bring it closer.

GYMKHANAS

Before taking a pony to a gymkhana it should be used to the sight of children jumping about in sacks, the sound of potatoes dropping into buckets, water being unexpectedly splashed on to it and all the other common, but alarming, happenings at these events.

I have seen accidents caused by all the things I have mentioned, and if a pony will not flinch at any of them, it is indeed 'shockproof', as every child's pony should be.

There are countless books on educating the child to the pony, but far too few on *educating the pony to the child.*

22

Why Not Breed a Foal?

M ANY people have a mare they would like to breed from, but owing to their lack of knowledge on the subject they dismiss the idea. If this applies to you, why not think again?

If you have a genuine interest in horses, average common sense and are willing to give up a little time to the care of a mare and foal then you have at least three of the requirements which are essential for a successful horse breeder.

SUITABLE LAND

Another is suitable land. Horses do best on fairly light, well-drained soil. Rich land suitable for fattening cattle is by no means the best for horses, as they prefer short, fine grass which is sweeter and more nutritious.

To encourage this type of herbage the pasture should be grazed bare by cattle and sheep up to the end of December. If there are rough patches of coarse grass and weeds cut them down, and treat the patches with agricultural salt. Weeds have no feeding value: they choke the finer grasses and are as detrimental on the land as they are in the garden. After the pasture has been grazed bare it should be harrowed. This cannot be overdone, so use a heavy, severe harrow. Leave the pasture empty until the spring, then roll it with a heavy roller, paying special attention to the patches where the weeds were. The roller will crush the fleshy roots, causing them to decay and nourish the finer grass.

The harrow loosens the soil and ventilates it, and also removes the dead herbage. Allow at least six weeks between harrowing and rolling so that the soil can take in all the oxygen it requires.

Do not use artificial manure on land intended for horses, but it will benefit from a dressing of basic slag every third or fourth year. This should be done in November, and five or six hundredweight to the acre is about the right quantity.

Good grass is essential for the healthy development of young horses, and no substitute is equally as good. The small outlay required to put the pasture in good heart will be money well spent, and will do much to reduce the hay and corn bill.

Whenever the grass is growing faster than the horses can graze it down, turn cattle out on it as well to help to keep it level.

Heavy, wet land is not suitable for horses, especially young stock, which will not thrive if they are forced to lie on cold, wet land. Shade, and shelter from the prevailing wind, is essential, and can best be provided by thick hedges, walls or trees. An open shed is an advantage in summer, when horses will use it to get away from the flies, but they will seldom go under it in winter, no matter how bad the weather may be. A good water supply is as important as good pasture. A fast-running stream or a water trough which is regularly cleaned out are both suitable. Never allow horses to drink from a stagnant pond or there will be great danger of them becoming infested with red worm.

Six or seven acres of good grazing is enough to keep two mares and their foals. It should be divided into three paddocks of similar size, which will make it possible to rest some of the pasture and keep the animals moving on to fresh grazing. Cattle must be turned on to the land from time to time or it will become horse-sick. A local farmer will usually welcome a little extra keep.

I

THE BEST TYPE OF ANIMAL TO BREED

Many people who have not previously bred horses will wish to breed a Thoroughbred or part Thoroughbred. I cannot advise them too strongly against this. Even with knowledge and experience it is not easy to breed a good horse of this type, and the market is always glutted with moderate or worthless animals of this kind. Thoroughbreds are seldom hardy enough to do well at grass all the year round, and they require skilled management from birth. It is far wiser to start with a breed or cross which is easy to rear, inexpensive to keep and likely to find a ready market. A good stamp of pony or cob is a much better proposition as they do well at grass throughout the year, which means a considerable saving in expense. The market for this type of animal is usually steady and lucrative.

THE BROOD MARE

Every mare is a potential brood mare, and you may already have a mare you would like to breed from. If she is old and a maiden the venture may prove not successful because she will probably be difficult to get in foal, and have a hard time foaling. A foal from an old maiden mare is often small and weakly and she may have very little milk for it. This is not always the case but the risk involved is hardly worth while. If, however, the mare has bred a foal in her younger days she may be successfully bred from at almost any age.

A brood mare should have reasonably good all-round conformation, and be free from hereditary unsoundness. Have her examined by a veterinary surgeon and ask his opinion of her suitability for a brood mare.

Now you must decide the best type of horse to send her to. The aim should always be to produce an animal with bone and substance combined with quality. A thirteen-hand pony of this stamp will carry either a child or an adult and there is always a demand for them. Likewise a good riding cob with quality and up to weight will find a ready market.

If your mare is between twelve and thirteen hands and a little short of bone she might produce a useful animal if she were put to a fourteen-hand Welsh cob of riding type. A coarse, cobby mare could breed a nice riding pony if crossed with an Arab or Anglo-Arab. If the mare is one of the pure native breeds it would be better to send her to a stallion of the same breed, providing you want the offspring to be about the same size as the dam. It is never wise to send a mare to a stallion which is more than two hands taller than herself. The crossing of animals which are vastly different in type should be avoided because it seldom produces good results.

Providing a mare is healthy and well grown she can be mated at three years old without detriment to her growth or development. She should be partly broken before she is covered, because an unbroken brood mare is difficult to handle at the time of foaling, and if the mother is wild the foal is sure to follow her example. It will do her no harm if her training is finished during the first few months of pregnancy, and she will be easier to school. Handle her with common sense, and do not gallop or school her over fences.

The gestation period is eleven months so the mare should be covered in May or June. The foal will then be dropped in April or May, which is the best time of year, because the temperature is less variable, the ground warmer and the new grass starting to grow. These conditions are ideal for the foal and will help the mare to provide ample milk.

A novice breeder should not try to get an early foal, because when grass is scarce both mare and foal will require skilled management, and the expense will be very much higher.

CARE OF A MARE IN FOAL

If your mare has been stabled all the winter, rough her off and turn her out at least a month before she is covered, otherwise she may be difficult to get in foal. She should not be fat, nor hard and dried up, and she will be all the better for living out while she is carrying a foal. Unless she is working keep her on fairly bare pasture so that she has to take exercise to get enough grass. When the grass loses its value, or if the mare is working, give her a small feed of damped oats and bran morning and evening. If she becomes over-fat she may have a difficult time foaling and the foal is likely to be small and weak.

During frost and snow keep the mare up entirely, but give her plenty of fresh air and do not coddle her. It is dangerous to turn a pregnant mare out on slippery ground: if she suddenly slips or falls she is liable to misplace the foal or lose it. It is also unwise to turn her out with young horses or geldings who may worry her and encourage her to gallop about.

Providing the weather is open she can live out all through the winter. Give her plenty of good hay and a small feed of oats and bran twice a day. A few roots and a linseed mash once a week will keep her bowels in good order.

Forget she is in foal during the first six months and work her in the usual way, but do not gallop her or allow her to become over-excited. If she is not working she must be turned out to exercise herself. During the eighth month and after she will only be fit for slow work, and cantering should be cut out. Light, unexciting work will do her no harm right up to the time of foaling. If you do not require her for work she must be turned out, and not allowed to become fat and idle.

A week or two before the mare is due to foal her udder will increase in size, especially if she is in at night, but it will go down considerably after exercise. Forty-eight hours before the foal is due she may become restless and uneasy, wandering about and rubbing her back against anything she can find. At this stage the udder will no longer fluctuate in size, and a waxy substance will usually form on the teats. When this drops off the mare can be expected to foal within twelve hours. These symptoms are usual but do not occur in every case. When foaling is imminent the muscles on either side of the backbone above the root of the tail will relax and fall in. Until this happens the foal cannot be born. When these hollows appear put the mare in a loose box which has been thoroughly cleaned and whitewashed, and the floor scrubbed with disinfectant. A foaling box should be at least fourteen-foot square, and have a door which opens outwards, otherwise the mare may lie down behind it. There should also be a peephole through which she can be observed without her knowing it. Bed the box down with clean, short straw which will not become entangled with the foal's feet.

FOALING

At the time of foaling the mare's bowels should be relaxed. To ensure this give her a linseed mash every other day for a fortnight before she is due, and half a pint of linseed oil when foaling is imminent.

Once hollows have appeared above the root of the tail the mare will usually foal within a few hours. Occasionally a mare will remain in this condition for several days. If this happens she must have exercise, so lead her out for half an hour four or five times a day.

When it is evident that the mare will foal shortly get in touch with your veterinary surgeon and make arrangements where you can contact him in case of need. Most mares foal without assistance and are far better if they are left alone and undisturbed. The foal will probably be born at night when everything is quiet. Some mares are very shy and will delay foaling for some hours if they think they are being observed, so keep out of sight as much as possible but remain within hearing.

Usually a mare will foal without difficulty or complications, but when they do arise skilled assistance must be called in without delay, or the result may be fatal to both mare and foal. The cause of a difficult foaling is nearly always malpresentation. This means that the foal is lying in a position which makes it impossible for it to pass through the pelvic circle. To change the position of a foal requires considerable knowledge, skill and strength, and should never be attempted by an inexperienced person. If prompt assistance is not forthcoming the foal may become firmly wedged in the pelvis, and the mare will continue to strain until her strength gives out; then little can be done to help her.

To avoid a situation of this kind you should know enough about a normal birth to recognize a complication should it occur. With this in mind I will explain the sequence of events in a normal foaling.

When labour starts the mare will wander round the box, paw the ground, stale and empty her bowels at frequent intervals, and strain occasionally. Once the pains become strong and regular, foaling should be complete within twenty minutes, or at most half an hour. After the appearance of the foal's muzzle the actual birth should not take more than ten minutes. The time factor is important because a mare, unlike a cow, will not stand up to protracted labour.

If the foal is in a normal position it will be lying on its belly, and the forefeet (one slightly in advance of the other) will appear first, followed almost immediately by the muzzle. Some mares foal standing up, but it is quite usual for them to lie down when the pains become strong. After the feet and head are born the deepest part of the foal's body will be entering the pelvis, and it will be a few minutes before the muscles expand sufficiently for it to pass through. At this stage the mare will show considerable distress. She will strain violently, groan, sweat and breathe heavily, but this is normal and need cause no alarm. Leave her alone for a few minutes and she will usually deliver her foal unaided. Unless it is evident that she is making no progress and the pains are growing weaker do not attempt to help her. Wait a few minutes as the passage may not be fully distended, and if help is given too soon the mare may be torn internally. The strength of the pains must be your guide; if they are strong do not interfere, but if you are certain they are growing weaker and no progress is being made, then she must be helped.

Tie a clean stable rubber round the foal's pasterns, and when the mare strains pull the forelegs downwards towards her hocks. Do not use a rope as it may damage the foal's pasterns. Keep one foot slightly in advance of the other so that both shoulders will not be forced through the pelvis at the same time. Never pull on the foal's legs unless the mare is straining, then pull downwards with a strong steady pressure, until the pain passes. Between pains hold the legs firmly so that they cannot recede. If the feet are level pull downwards as described, but first to one side and then to the other in order to get one shoulder through the pelvis at a time. Once the shoulders are born there should be no further trouble, and the birth will be complete in a few minutes.

CARE OF THE FOAL AFTER BIRTH

Up to the time of birth the foal is encased in a bag of fluid. This usually breaks when the feet appear. If the mare foals standing up the foal will slide gently over her hocks to the ground, and in doing so the navel cord will be broken. But if the mare foals lying down, then the cord may have to be cut. Use a pair of large scissors which have been boiled in water and disinfectant. Leave them in it until they are required. Cut the cord two or three inches from the foal's body. Until it has dried up and dropped off there is always a danger that the foal may develop Joint Evil. This is a crippling and usually fatal disease caused by a germ which enters the body through the navel cord. If the cord is tied the risk of infection is reduced; on the other hand this is an unnatural practice which prevents the cord from draining, and sometimes causes trouble of another nature. The opinion of experienced breeders are divided on this subject, so it would be better to consult your veterinary surgeon and follow his advice. At the same time ask him to recommend a suitable disinfectant to dress the cord, and to syringe out the mare's vagina if necessary.

Immediately the foal is born examine its muzzle and make

sure that its nostrils are not obstructed by membrane from the placenta. If they are, remove it without delay or the foal will die from suffocation. Once the cord is broken the foal is dependent on its own lungs for air. Watch it carefully and make sure it is breathing. If not, prompt action must be taken to promote respiration. Open the foal's mouth and gently pull its tongue forward, then blow hard down its throat and up its nostrils and release its tongue. If it does not gasp and draw air into its lungs repeat the process until it does. Splashing cold water in the foal's face and slapping its chest with a cold, wet towel will also help to start respiration. Most foals start to breathe of their own accord, but it is easy to lose one for want of a little timely aid.

If the mare is lying down pull the foal round to her head, and place it where she can reach it, but do not put it directly in front of her forelegs or she may damage it in getting up. Remove the soiled straw, and then if the mare seems all right and is licking the foal leave them alone together.

If the foal is strong and healthy it will soon try to get up; usually making several efforts before gaining its legs. Do not help it unless it gets cast against a wall, then pull it clear so that it has room to get its forelegs out in front in order to rise. If it falls between the mare's legs leave the box at once—she will not step on it unless she becomes upset and worried.

When the foal is up it will nose about until it finds the mare's udder, and it should be sucking within two hours of birth. If it is too weak to get up it must be helped. This is best done by two people, standing facing each other, one on either side of it. Lift it gently to its feet and steady it by supporting its weight. Propel it towards the mare's flank and encourage it to find the udder for itself. If it is unable to do so, draw a little milk on to your finger and give it to the foal to suck, then move your hand towards the mare's udder until the foal's nose rests against it, and try to substitute a teat for your finger. Try not to frighten the foal or make it struggle. If it is too weak to feed this way, you will have to milk the mare and feed the foal from a bottle. Draw the milk into a bowl and transfer it to a baby's bottle. Stand this in hot water until the milk is blood heat before giving it to the foal. Feed the foal every two hours until it is strong enough to get up and suck for itself. It is important to sterilize the bowl and bottle before each feed. The mare's first milk is extremely beneficial to the foal, so do not make the mistake of giving it cow's milk because it is easier.

A foal should empty its bowels within an hour of first sucking. If it repeatedly tries to do so but passes nothing, it must receive attention, as constipation is often fatal if it is neglected. To do this, vaseline your middle finger, making sure your hands are clean and nails short. Insert it into the foal's rectum and gently remove any dung you can feel. If the straining continues without result give the foal an enema of half a pint of lukewarm water and a dessert-spoonful of glycerine. Repeat every hour until the bowel is empty. If this treatment is not successsful give the foal a little castor oil. Keep the action of the bowels under observation for at least a month.

Most foals are strong and healthy, needing neither help nor treatment, and are better left alone with the mare as much as possible for the first few days.

CARE OF THE MARE AFTER FOALING

By the time you have seen to the foal and removed the soiled bedding, the mare will probably be on her feet. If so give her a bucket of chilled water with a little linseed tea in it and a warm bran mash with a pound of crushed oats added. If she feels cold to the touch and appears exhausted put a rug on her and a set of wool bandages on her legs, and massage her ears until they are warm. A quart of strong, black coffee is a good stimulant, but should only be given if the mare appears very exhausted. After two hours give her a second mash and a net of good hay. For a few days her food should be relaxing and include plenty of fresh green fodder.

Usually a mare will cleanse (expel the afterbirth) within an hour of foaling, but if she has not done so within five hours inform your veterinary surgeon. This seldom happens, but if the afterbirth is retained the result may be fatal.

Shortly after foaling the mare may show signs of pain, and strain a little; this is caused by the normal contraction of the internal muscles and it will pass off. In rare cases straining may be violent and continuous. This is a dangerous condition and should receive prompt veterinary attention, or the mare may damage herself internally.

Do not allow the afterbirth to trail on the ground. Tie a knot in it and shorten it to the level of the hocks.

An evil-smelling discharge from the vagina is usually due to internal tearing. Syringe out the vagina twice a day with warm water and a mild disinfectant until the condition clears up.

Do not think that the whole business of breeding a foal is beset with hazards. This is definitely not the case. Most mares foal quickly, need no help and give little trouble. But when skilled help is necessary it must be sought without delay.

Before your mare foals the following points should be memorized:

BEFORE FOALING

(a) Thoroughly clean, whitewash and disinfect the foaling box.

(b) Ensure the mare's bowels are relaxed.

(c) Anyone attending the mare must wear a clean overall, scrub their hands in disinfectant and cut their nails short.

(d) Arrange in advance where you can contact your vet in case of need. Ask advice on how to treat the navel cord, and the best disinfectant to use.

(e) You will require: large sharp scissors, thin tape (if cord is to be tied), disinfectant, enema (human size), vaseline, glycerine, castor oil, linseed oil, several clean stable rubbers, hand towel, soap and plenty of hot water.

FOALING

(a) Normal presentation: both forefeet, followed almost immediately by the muzzle.
(b) If both hind feet appear first the foal will probably be born without assistance.
(c) If the foal is presented in any other way send for a vet without delay.
(d) A normal birth should not take more than half an hour.

CARE OF THE FOAL AT BIRTH

(a) Examine the muzzle at once and make sure that the nostrils are not obstructed.
(b) To promote respiration, pull the tongue forward and blow down the throat. Repeat if necessary.
(c) The foal should be on its feet and sucking within two hours of birth, and empty its bowels shortly after feeding.

CARE OF MARE AFTER FOALING

(a) For exhaustion give a quart of strong, black coffee. Put on a rug and a set of wool bandages. Rub ears until warm.
(b) Call in veterinary surgeon if mare does not cleanse within five hours of foaling.
(c) Leave the mare and foal alone and undisturbed as much as possible for the first forty-eight hours after foaling.

Plan in advance and have everything ready before the mare is due to foal.

23

Management of Mare and Foal

IF A foal is strong and the weather mild and dry it can go out to grass with the mare when it is three days old. A young foal's eyesight is very poor, so put a head collar on it and lead it behind the mare. Keep it close to her and try not to frighten it. The foal can be loose in the paddock, but let the mare graze on a leading rein for the first two days, or she may gallop about before the foal has got its bearings. If the foal scampers about and gets lost, take the mare to it; do not try to drive it to her. Be careful that the foal's legs do not become entangled with the leading rein. When it begins to get tired take them both in. After two or three days they can both be turned out loose. A young foal is very susceptible to chill from cold wind and damp, so until it is a month old bring it in if the weather is unfavourable. After that it can stay out night and day providing the weather is reasonably warm.

Give the mare a feed of damped oats and bran mixed with a little chaff twice a day, and encourage the foal to share it with her. If it is accustomed to a manger feed of this kind from the start it will not suffer a setback when it is weaned. Neither will it become pot-bellied from indigestion owing to being put on to food to which it is unaccustomed.

A mare usually comes into season nine days after she has foaled. If you intend to breed from her the following year this is the best time to have her covered, as it is usually a fertile heat. If you wish her to foal at the stud where the stallion stands, this can be arranged, and she should be sent there at least a month before the foal is due.

When a mare is in season her milk often becomes a little acid, and this may cause the foal to scour slightly. This should pass off quickly and need cause no concern, but if it continues for several days give the foal a small dose of castor oil to clear out whatever is upsetting its stomach. Apply Vaseline to the under surface of the tail to prevent scalding.

If at any time the foal develops diarrhoea of a watery, brown nature, goes off its food and appears ill, isolate it at once and inform your veterinary surgeon. This type of diarrhoea is highly infectious and should not be treated lightly.

WEANING

If the mare is pregnant, wean the foal when it is seven months old, otherwise it can continue to run with her and weaning will be a gradual process as she loses her milk. If the foal is to be weaned at seven months, put it and the mare in a loose box overnight; next morning take the mare from the foal, and if possible remove her out of earshot. The foal will not fret so much if it is left alone in a loose box it is used to. If you have two foals wean them at the same time and put them together for company. Otherwise keep the foal shut in for a couple of days and then turn it out with some young cattle. Without company of any kind a foal will fret and go back in condition. When it is first weaned it should have six pounds of crushed oats, two pounds of bran and four pounds of chaff a day. Mix it all together and divide it into four or five small feeds a day, which should be fed slightly damp. Gradually reduce the number of feeds to two or three a day, but do not reduce the total quantity. For the first two years of its life a foal should be fed really well, as it makes most of its growth during this time. At three years old growth will be slower and the animal will be better able to fend for itself. In summer good grazing will supply all his needs, but this must be supplemented with a liberal ration of oats and good seed hay in winter.

Always keep young horses under close observation so that any setback will be noticed and put right before the animal has had time to deteriorate to any extent.

Every foal *must* be treated for worms or it will soon become unthrifty. The best time to do this is a month or six weeks after it is weaned. Suitable worm powders can be obtained from any veterinary chemist.

Teach the foal to lead in hand when it is very young. Handle it firmly and gently and try not to frighten it. A foal which has been badly frightened at an early age often grows into a sulky, difficult horse. It should also become accustomed to being handled all over, and having its feet picked up. These should be trimmed whenever necessary as overgrown feet put abnormal strain on joints and tendons, and may cause permanent unsoundness. Teeth should also be examined from time to time, because the surface of the back teeth may become uneven and prevent the animal from grinding its food properly.

A young horse should progress steadily from the time he is foaled, and care must be taken that he does not stand still during the winter months due to insufficient body-building food. A young horse is very susceptible to red worm, and these parasites will play havoc with his constitution, so have his droppings tested every six months.

Do not be disappointed if a good-looking yearling turns into a plain two-year-old; he will probably regain his good looks when he is a three-year-old. A youngster often grows first at one end and then the other, so it is often impossible to judge what his final conformation will be like until he is four years old. A horse which is very big at this age may be extremely backward and may not be fully developed until he is six.

CARE OF THE MARE AFTER THE FOAL IS WEANED

The mare will need special care for a short time after the foal is weaned, especially if she has a lot of milk. Cut her food and water down for a few days to reduce the flow. Keep her in and give her dry food only. If her udder becomes hard and full, draw a little milk from it two or three times a day, but do not milk her out. It should not be necessary to do this for more than a week, and during this time she will benefit from light work. If her udder is hard and painful, foment it with warm water, then draw off most of the milk and rub it with olive oil. A mild dose of physic will help to dry her off. She should be turned out on rather bare pasture for a time, otherwise the milk may return.

Few things are more interesting than to plan the breeding of a foal, and then to watch it progress and develop. To be a successful breeder you must have an elementary knowledge of the complications and difficulties which may arise, but you should not be put off by these adverse possibilities. In practice you will find that mares usually foal quickly and easily and seldom require any help. With a little knowledge and experience it is not difficult to breed strong, healthy stock which will afford you great personal satisfaction, and find a ready and profitable market.

It is accepted that the following are hereditary diseases and that it is unwise to breed from parents suffering from any one of them: Ringbone; Cataract; Roaring; Whistling; Sidebone; Bone Spavin; Navicular; Shivering; Stringhalt; Parrot-mouth.

24

'Horsecellaneous'

I. CARE OF LEGS AFTER HUNTING

Hunting exposes a horse's legs to the risk of many minor injuries such as scratches, cuts, puncture wounds, thorns, abrasions, bruises and minor strains. If they are neglected any of these seemingly slight injuries may cause lameness and lay a horse off for some time. Such slight injuries are often difficult to detect because they cause no unsoundness until some complication arises.

If the following treatment is given as a matter of routine after hunting the majority of these injuries will heal without causing further trouble.

When the horse's legs are dry and clean, and have been examined for thorns, apply a set of hot soda bandages, and a set of dry wool bandages on top to keep the heat in.

To prepare soda bandages, dissolve one pound of washing soda in a gallon of boiling water. Immerse a set of loosely rolled wool bandages in this and leave them to soak until they are cool enough to handle. Make sure that the solution has penetrated to the centre of the bandages, then wring out most of the surplus water. Apply them to the legs comfortably hot and roll on fairly loosely. Put a set of dry bandages on top to conserve the heat.

The soda is a mild astringent and very penetrating, and will take much of the inflammation and soreness out of bruises and strains. Blood is nature's greatest healer and the heat will draw it to any part which is injured. Leave the bandages on over night.

If soda bandages are routine treatment after hunting, a horse will seldom 'miss his turn' through complications arising from minor injuries.

2. THE PROBABLE CAUSE OF A HORSE AT GRASS GOING WRONG IN THE WIND

An owner is often afraid to turn a valuable horse out to grass in the summer in case he goes wrong in his wind. This is by no means an uncommon occurrence, especially in horses over sixteen hands, and is usually due to the sudden change of food.

During the hunting season a horse is usually fed on a large quantity of highly concentrated food, and his system becomes accustomed to it.

Grass contains a large percentage of water, so the horse has to consume an abnormal amount in an attempt to get the concentrates his system is missing. As a result the stomach becomes distended and presses on the diaphragm, which in turn presses on the lungs and impedes their action. Over a long period this may permanently impair them. This can be avoided if, when the horse is first turned out, he is given three-quarters of his usual ration of concentrates, divided into two feeds a day. Cut the amount down gradually as he becomes accustomed to the change of diet. If the horse is given a small daily ration of corn right through the summer he will be much easier to get fit when he is brought up. To prevent him becoming too fat bring him in during the daytime when the flies are at their worst.

If this practice is followed the risk of a horse going wrong in his wind at grass is negligible.

3. TO STOP BLEEDING

If a blood-vessel is torn or severed place a shilling over the site of injury. Keep it in position with a pressure pad and firm

K

bandage. This is only a temporary measure to tide over an emergency. Have the wound properly dressed by a veterinary surgeon as soon as possible. Do not use a copper or nickel coin.

4. TO PROMOTE WARMTH

If a horse is thoroughly chilled from exposure, exhaustion or debility, warmth and circulation will be improved by placing a hot-water bottle between the blanket and the rug in a position over the heart on either side of the body. Put the roller on so that it holds them in position. This will help to warm the blood as it leaves the heart and so improve the circulation.

If the legs are cold give them a brisk friction rub with a stable rubber, and apply a set of wool bandages which have been previously heated in the oven. Also hand-rub the ears until they are warm. This treatment is also excellent in cases of severe shock.

5. TO IMPROVE FEET WITH POOR OR BRITTLE HORN

If your horse has weak, brittle feet apply a mild blister round the coronet. When this has cleared up have a set of lawn-mowing boots made for him, which are a half-inch bigger all round than the size of his feet. From the kennels or a knacker's yard get three or four pounds of horse fat. Render this down and mix it with half a pound of Stockholm Tar and an ounce of common salt, and then stir in two pounds of bran. Place a layer of this mixture at the bottom of one of the boots then put it on the horse and pack more of the mixture round the sides so that it covers all the wall of the foot. Treat the other feet in the same way. Do not remove the boots for ten days. Continue to dress the horse's feet with Stockholm Tar and horse fat until such time as the feet have become normal and the walls sound. Any fat which is not horse fat is useless, and of course the shoes must be removed before the treatment is started.

6. NAVICULAR DISEASE

At one time this disease was incurable, but it can now be cured in the early stages by cortizone injections. Many advanced cases have also responded to this treatment.

7. A TEST FOR SPLINT LAMENESS

If a splint cannot be felt it is often difficult to diagnose lameness, from this cause. The following method, although not infallible, is a useful guide. Lift the unsound leg and bring the foot up to the elbow. Place the hand under the cannon bone and press it up as close to the forearm as possible. Hold it there for a full minute, keeping as much upward pressure on it as you can, then release it, and immediately have the horse run out in hand. If he goes sound for a few strides the lameness is nearly always due to a splint—probably a knee splint.

8. TO PREVENT GIRTH GALLS

A young horse or one which has been running out at grass for some time will be in soft condition and liable to develop girth-galls when first put into work. To prevent this, harden the skin by applying either surgical spirit or a strong solution of salt-and-water to the parts where galls are likely to appear. It will also help to prevent galls if the girth is passed through an old inner tube. (Motor-bike size.) Keep the girth or girths scrubbed clean, as dried sweat is a frequent cause of galling.

9. COLIC

If a colic drench is not available give the horse a dessert spoonful of bicarbonate of soda to a pint of warm water as a drench. This will often break up and dispel the internal gasses. For a horse which is subject to colic after hunting add a dessert spoonful of bicarbonate of soda to his bran mash. This will sometimes prevent an attack of colic.

10. TO KEEP THE STOMACH AND KIDNEYS FREE FROM ACIDITY

Add a level dessert spoonful of washing soda to the drinking water two or three times a week.

11. EXHAUSTION

A quart of warm, strong black coffee given as a drench is an excellent stimulant for a horse suffering from exhaustion due to exposure, fatigue, debility or after a difficult foaling.

12. TO DETECT A 'SQUEAK'

A roarer or a whistler is not likely to get by undetected, but it is quite a different matter if a horse makes an almost imperceptible 'squeak'. As a rule this type of wind unsoundness cannot be heard when the horse is galloping, but it is sometimes apparent at a walk, but more often when the animal is trotting or cantering slowly in a tight circle.

If you are testing a horse for his wind always ride him in a snaffle. Some horses make a noise due to bridle contraction in a double bridle, and this will make it impossible to hear any slight sound caused by a wind infirmity. If you can hear nothing when he is moving, give him a brisk canter, then jump off and encourage him to stretch his neck, and listen carefully to his breathing. It is sometimes possible to hear a slight whistle as he stretches his neck.

An owner will often mention that his horse makes a noise, and then add that it does not effect his performance in any way. Take this with a grain of salt. If a horse is wrong in his wind the condition will get worse, and sooner or later he will become useless.

13. ACONITE POWDERS

These are a good all-round tonic, and especially beneficial to a horse which is unsound in his wind. They will not cure this defect, but often prolong his working life. Aconite is a poison, so do not give a larger dose than prescribed on the packet.

14. MOULDY HAY

This often affects a horse's lungs, and is a common cause of broken wind.

15. WOUNDS

These should never be neglected, and acriflavine is an excellent dressing for all clean wounds, especially chipped or broken knees, as it helps to prevent the formation of proud flesh or granulation. A kaolin poultice should be applied to all septic wounds.

16. TREATMENT FOR COLDS

Add a teaspoonful of eucalyptus oil to a pint of boiling water. Soak a handful of hay in this and place it at the bottom of a nose-bag. Put the nose-bag on the horse's head so that he is obliged to inhale the fumes.

If you have no nose-bag, add a tablespoonful of eucalyptus to a pint of boiling water and sprinkle it all over the bedding in the horse's box, then shut the door and windows up and leave him to inhale the fumes for two or three hours. Normal ventilation should then be restored.

A horse suffering from a cold will benefit from plenty of fresh air. If the weather is severe put an extra blanket on him. Never shut him up in a stuffy loose box. It will help to clear the discharge from the nose if the feed and hay is placed on the ground. If the horse has a sore throat or a cough give him a good electuary which can be bought at any veterinary chemist.

17. TO PREVENT A HORSE TEARING HIS CLOTHING

Stitch thick leather over the parts he tears. If this does not prove successful, stitch two pieces of stiff leather on to the noseband of the head collar at the sides above the corners of the mouth. They should come well below the level of the lips, and be wide enough to prevent the horse catching the rug in his teeth no matter which way he twists his head. This will not prevent him feeding, and if the leather guards are worn over a long period the horse may forget the habit.

18. BOX WALKING

A horse cannot indulge in this habit if bales of straw are placed in his loose box in such a way that he can move about and lie down but cannot walk round and round.

19. BLINKERS

If blinkers are put on a horse which is difficult to clip, shoe or load into a horse box, it will often have a quieting effect.

20. TO MAKE A HORSE WALK

Some horses constantly jog instead of walking. To stop this tiresome habit, take a piece of loose skin on the shoulder between your finger and thumb and twist it until the horse walks. As you do so say 'Walk', and as soon as he does, release the pressure. Do this every time he jogs and in time he may give up the habit.

21. TO PREVENT A HORSE EATING HIS BEDDING

Disolve two or three ounces of bitter aloes in half a gallon of hot water and sprinkle it over the bedding.

22. WATERING

When a horse is watered three or four times a day, always allow him to drink all he requires, and do not remove the bucket as soon as he lifts his head. Many horses pause several times before they have had enough, and if the bucket is removed before he has finished drinking he will never get all the water he needs. Poor condition is often caused by insufficient water. Deep 'poverty' marks down the quarters, on either side of the tail, is another sign that a horse is not getting enough to drink.

23. HORSE-NUTS OR CUBES

These should be fed in place of oats if a horse is inclined to get overfresh and above himself in spite of an adequate amount of work. This is an excellent feed for young horses during breaking and also for children's ponies. It is a scientifically balanced ration and can entirely replace oats.

24. BEANS

Beans are one of the best energy-producing foods. A half a pint of *old* split beans added to the morning feed will help an old horse to stand up to a long day's hunting. They can also be fed with advantage to horses turned out to grass during the winter. They must be at least two years old and fed split or cracked. Do not feed them regularly to young horses which are stabled as they are too heating.

25. A METHOD OF USING THE CURB ON A PELHAM BIT

A Pelham will afford better control if the ends of the curb-chain are passed through the snaffle rings before being placed on the hooks.

26. FOR A HARD OR ONE-SIDED MOUTH

Bind one side of a snaffle from the ring to the centre joint with a piece of strong, hard string about as thick as a match. Bind the bit carefully so that each circle of string lies against the previous one. A saddler will show you the correct way to secure the end of the string.

A bit bound in this way will usually prevent a horse taking a strong hold. If one side of the mouth is insensitive, bind the bit on this side. The same method can be used on a bar bit. Do not bind more than one side of a bit or the effect will be negative.

27. A BIT FOR A FOUR-YEAR-OLD

In a class for show hunters a double bridle might be termed a 'uniform'. Owing to this 'fashion' a four-year-old is usually shown in a double bridle regardless of the fact that his mouth may not be ready for it. The mouth of a young horse is often ruined in this way, but it can be overcome to a great extent by the use of a short-cheek Banbury bit. Bits of this kind are made with a cheek no more than an inch long, and are known as 'Tom Thumbs'. This bit has a sliding mouth-piece, and most youngsters take kindly to it. The action of the curb is very mild so there is little risk of the horse becoming over-bent.

28. AN ADDITION TO A BREAKING BIT

Unless a young horse will play with his bit it is impossible to make his mouth, but it is not uncommon for a youngster to sulk with his bit and make no attempt to move it about in his mouth. If keys do not encourage him to play with it make a fairly thick tassel from mane or tail hair, and attach it to the centre of the bit and adjust it low in the horse's mouth. If this does not produce the desired result, smear the tassel with black treacle. Most horses like this and in order to get it off will play about with the bit.

29. THE DROPPED NOSEBAND

If your horse takes a strong hold the use of a severe bit will only deaden his mouth, and in the end make matters worse. It is far better to use a snaffle in conjunction with a dropped noseband. There are many types on the market and it is usually possible to find one that will suit your horse, no matter what his peculiarity may be.

The efficiency of any dropped noseband depends on correct fitting. Avoid thin nosebands, these cut into a horse's nose like a piece of string.

30. TO SOFTEN LEATHER

To soften the flaps of a saddle which has been neglected or badly stored apply a generous coating of Neat's Foot oil to the under surface of the flaps. Allow it to soak in for twenty-four hours, then roll the flaps from the bottom upwards; release them, and repeat until the leather becomes pliable. Allow another coating of oil to soak in, then repeat the process. If the under surface of the leather is oiled before the saddle is stored it will preserve it and prevent the leather from becoming hard and cracking.

A folded leather girth can be kept soft by pouring a little Neat's Foot oil on the inner lining.

31. HIND SHOES

These are not usually necessary for a native-bred pony unless it is constantly working on the road. However, its hind feet should be kept under constant observation, and if the walls show excessive wear the pony will have to be shod.

32. INEXPENSIVE LITTER FOR AN EXERCISE RING

If weeds, rank grass, leaves and other garden refuse are dried and stacked they will make a suitable covering for an exercise ring when the ground is too hard to exercise a horse anywhere else. Do not include trimmings from shrubs as many of these are poisonous to horses.

33. RED WORM

Young horses at grass are particularly subject to these parasites, especially if they drink from a pond. Always suspect red worm if a young horse lies down a great deal, and appears to have difficulty in rising. It is a wise precaution to have the droppings tested for red worm in spring and autumn. More young horses die through the effects of red worm than from any other single cause.

34. AN EXTRA BLANKET

In very cold weather this is almost equivalent to an extra pound of corn a day, because it will promote warmth without drawing it from what the horse eats.

35. CLOTHING

Do not weigh a horse down with a lot of heavy, poor quality clothing. In normal winter weather two wool blankets and a good rug should be ample. A set of wool bandages often do more to keep a horse warm than an extra rug.

36. WEEDS

To keep horse pastures in good order scythe down all patches of weeds and rank grass. Do not leave them lying on the ground; rake them up and burn them right away. Although horses will not eat them when they are growing, they will often gorge themselves on this kind of rubbish when it is half withered—sometimes with fatal results.

37. DANGER OF HAY NETS FOR PONIES

When hanging up a full net of hay for a pony make sure it will be high enough when it is empty to prevent the animal from pawing at it and putting its foot through the mesh. If a pony gets its foot fast in a hay net it can cause a serious accident, and possibly a broken leg.

38. SAFETY PRECAUTIONS

If you are turning a horse loose in a field take the precaution of turning his hind quarters towards the pasture. Stand by his head and when you let him go, step back away from him. If he gallops off with a flourish of heels you will be out of range, whereas if you allow him to face the field, his body will have to pass you as he goes away, and if he kicks you will probably be on the receiving end.

The same method should be used when lunging a horse. Turn him so that he faces you, then step back from him before sending him into a circle.

39. ELECTRIC FENCING

This is not suitable fencing for horse pastures unless the animals are very quiet and placid. Those that revel in a good gallop will, sooner or later, go straight through it—probably with disastrous results.

40. THE VOICE OF EXPERIENCE!

A very small boy once told me he had learned all about horses, so I asked him what he knew. He replied that they had four dangerous legs, and there was always something the matter with them.

It has taken me over half a century to discover just how *right he was*!

TO STOP BLEEDING—With the advent of new decimal currency it is safer not to use a coin of any kind but to rely on the pressure pad as a temporary measure. RED WORM—This parasite exists in all horse pastures and all horses carry a certain red-worm burden. Since the cycle of the worm is approximately six weeks it is advisable that young horses, which will not have developed the resistance found in older ones, should be wormed at more frequent intervals than stated but, of course, under veterinary supervision. Ed.

Index

Compiled by F. D. Buck

Page references in italics indicate an illustration